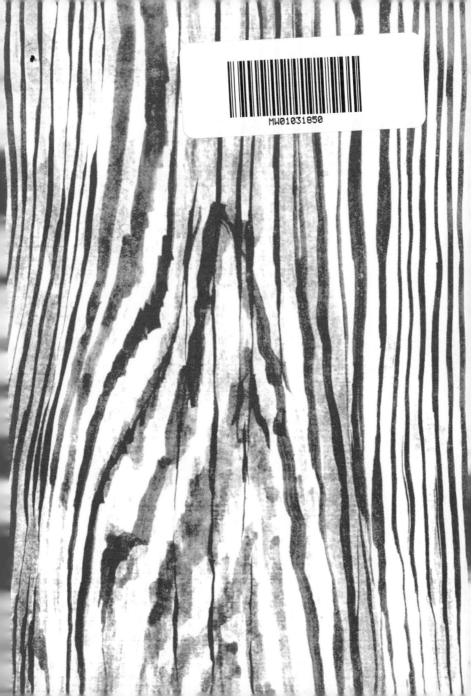

MW01031850

FIFTY

THINGS

TO DO WITH A

STICK

Pavilion
An imprint of HarperCollins*Publishers* Ltd
1 London Bridge Street
London SE1 9GF

www.harpercollins.co.uk

HarperCollins*Publishers*
1st Floor, Watermarque Building
Ringsend Road Dublin 4
Ireland

10 9 8 7 6 5 4 3 2 1

First published in Great Britain by Pavilion, an
imprint of HarperCollins*Publishers* Ltd 2022

MIX
Paper from
responsible sources
FSC **FSC® C007454**
www.fsc.org

This book is produced from independently
certified FSC™ paper to ensure responsible
forest management.

For more information visit:
www.harpercollins.co.uk/green

Printed and bound in China.

IMPORTANT SAFETY NOTICE

This book includes activities and projects that inherently include the risk of injury or
damage. We cannot guarantee that following the activities or projects in this book is
safe for everyone. For this reason, this book is sold without warranties or guarantees
of any kind, expressed or implied, and the publisher and the author disclaim any
liability for injuries, losses and damages caused in any way by the content of this
book. The publisher and author urge the reader to thoroughly review each activity
and to understand the use of all tools before beginning any project. Use and enjoy
fire safely and responsibly. Always check that you have permission to use the land
where the activities or projects take place. Children should always be supervised
when undertaking any activity or project in this book.

FIFTY

THINGS

TO DO WITH A

STICK

Richard Skrein

Illustrations by Maria Nilsson

PAVILION

Contents

Introduction

A seed drops from its mother tree. Nestled in the earth, it absorbs water and tentative roots begin to grow. Tiny at first, these roots lock the seed in place. No matter how far it has travelled to get to this point, the seed has now found its home.

A shoot emerges and moves towards the sun, forming a first leaf when it finds its way above ground. Grazing mammals and walkers' boots pose a threat to this fragile sapling's existence, but up it rises to become a small tree. It grows side shoots – branches – each one a fractal pattern that maps the tree's life story as it stretches for light and survival in its own unique ecosystem.

The tree thickens and spreads. It wants to grow, but breaking apart is built into this natural rhythm; an expression of the cycles of life, death, renewal and rebirth that encircle us all. A branch snaps off in high winds. A knot will form on the trunk – a reminder of what once grew there. The branch falls to the forest floor and lies among the leaf litter. That's when we come along …

'A stick!'

It can be any thing to any person. The ultimate open-ended object – a catapult, walking stick and everything in between. This book is an invitation to explore the countless possibilities for the wood that has found its way into your hands.

Playing with sticks is a simple expression of the connection between us and the natural world, and our place within it. Connect with that *more-than-human* world and you may just become hardwired to protect it – finding beauty, meaning, reverence and joy along the way.

Now … let's go and play!

Ecological impact

The projects in this book invite you to go out and gather natural resources. It's important that we reflect on our impact on the land and consider how we will minimize it while honouring the gifts that the natural world has given us. Each of us will interpret this in our own way. The following quote beautifully expresses one such way to do that.

Know the ways of the ones who take care of you, so that you may take care of them.
Introduce yourself. Be accountable as the one who comes asking for life.
Ask permission before taking. Abide by the answer.
Never take the first. Never take the last.
Take only what you need.
Take only that which is given.
Never take more than half. Leave some for others.
Harvest in a way that minimizes harm.
Use it respectfully. Never waste what you have taken.
Share.
Give thanks for what you have been given.
Give a gift, in reciprocity for what you have taken.
Sustain the ones who sustain you and the earth will last forever.

Robin Wall Kimmerer
Braiding Sweetgrass: Indigenous Wisdom, Scientific Knowledge and the Teachings of Plants

Tree species

A stick is not 'just a stick'. As discussed in the introduction, the life story of its mother tree will have literally shaped each branch in its own unique way. Furthermore, the species from which it came will determine its characteristics and potential uses.

For this book, I will extend the definition of a stick from 'a thin piece of wood that has fallen or been cut from a tree' to include larger branches, logs and bark. We'll also work with other interesting materials along the way.

In this section, we will look at a selection of tree species. The discussion of each species will highlight the properties of the wood and how those qualities lend themselves to the projects in this book.

We will also pause for a moment on each species to honour some of the history, folklore and traditional beliefs associated with particular trees.

This list is not exhaustive and there are many wonderful books that go into finer detail. I also advise you to research your local trees, plants and fungi – in particular those with poisonous elements such as the raw berries of the elder tree.

Common beech
(*Fagus sylvatica*)

A great mother beech tree (one of the oldest and largest) is a sight to behold, and a beech forest in autumn is like nowhere else. I have a soft spot for this tree and its monumental, bulging, twisting trunk and vast canopy.

Its wood is strong and durable and so it is useful for tool handles and kitchen utensils, among other things.

It is said that the English word 'book' comes from '*bok*', the Anglo-Saxon name for beech. Writing was carved on thin slices of beech to make early examples of the pages you now hold.

Silver birch
(*Betula pendula*)

With fluffy, swinging branches in the canopy and a long, thin trunk dressed in black and white, the birch tree is beautiful. The attractive bark works well for weaving projects such as the bark pots (page 56) and for those where you would leave the wood with the bark on to show off the smooth white-silver zebra markings (see the pencil pot on page 63).

Birch is prized by outdoor people for the flammable oils in the outer bark, which make it an excellent fire starter. It is softer than other hardwoods so it is useful for woodworking projects and great for beginners to work with. As birches tend to live fast and die young, you may be more likely to find recently fallen trees ready for harvesting.

As a pioneer species, birch is often one of the first to move into a new landscape and pave the way for the rest of the forest to follow. This association between the birch and new beginnings is reflected in Celtic mythology. As the first tree of the Ogham, the Celtic tree alphabet, it represents renewal and purification across many Celtic festivals and practices.

Further east, ancient Slavs would hug a birch to bring luck, power and joy. The trees have also been praised and celebrated across Russian literature, folk sayings and songs across the years.

Common ash
(*Fraxinus excelsior*)

Smooth barked as a young tree, rough and fissured in later life, the ash has feathered leaves and bunches of seeds hanging like sets of keys from its branches. In winter, it can be identified by its distinctive black, velvety buds.

Solid, long-lasting and attractive, ash wood is prized for tool handles, furniture and longbows. Older ash trees will have a distinctively darker heartwood running through the centre.

Ash is ring porous (it has large open pores in its rings) and so is not used for vessels or spoons.

In Norse mythology, the great world tree Yggdrasil was an ash that grew to the heavens, whose branches spread out across all places and within which many fantastical tales occurred. Indeed, the Norse god Odin possessed a spear made of ash, as did Achilles in Homer's epic poem, *The Iliad*.

Elder
(*Sambucus nigra*)

Elder is a small tree or shrub that grows no higher than 15 metres (and often a lot less). Its bark is corky and its leaves are feathered. In the summer, you'll find it festooned with white, highly scented flowers, followed by purple-black berries later on. It's often found near badger setts and rabbit warrens as the animals distribute the seeds in their droppings. Do note that, although the flowers and cooked berries are edible, the other parts of the plant – including the uncooked berries – are poisonous to humans.

Mature elder wood can be used for carving and whittling. The younger stems are useful for their soft, pithy core that can be hollowed out to make beads and tubes (pages 68–71).

The tree is positively dripping in folklore and mythology. It is said to be inhabited by a powerful spirit – the Elder Mother. We must seek permission from her if we are to harvest even the smallest branch. Popular superstition tells us that if we burn elder we will see the devil, but an elder planted outside the house will keep him away.

In the Christian tradition, it is said that Judas Iscariot hanged himself from an elder after betraying Jesus. *Cercis siliquastrum*, the Judas tree, also lays claim to this dark infamy. The choice of these species is thought to be a sly comment on the stature of Judas – neither is a tall or strong tree. Conversely, it has also been said that the death of Judas on the elder is the very reason it is often now limited in size to a scrubby bush. Indeed, he even makes a reappearance every autumn, or more specifically his ears do … *Auricularia auricula-judae,* or 'Judas's ear', is an ear-shaped fungus that favours elder wood.

English oak
(*Quercus robur*)

Regarded by many to be the 'King of the Woods', the oak has a reputation for strength and majesty. Its thick trunk is wrapped in fissured and cracked bark, while its canopy reaches out in every direction, decorated with artistically lobed leaves and green acorns.

Oak is well-regarded for some woodworking, such as fences, shingles and furniture, as it splits well and is durable. It is, however, very hard to carve and whittle. It's also best to avoid oak for making kitchen utensils due to its large pores and high levels of tannic acid. Oak will make a good chopping block, especially a nice knotty round.

The oak has a rich history of folkloric associations across the globe: an oak tree sheltered Zeus at birth in Arcadia; early kings in Western Europe wore oak-leaf crowns; and the wise and satyric Green Man, an ancient pagan symbol depicting a face surrounded by oak leaves, can still be found today peering out from stonework and stained glass across the United Kingdom.

Hazel
(*Corylus avellana*)

Hazel can often be found in distinctive thick nests of long, straight shoots that grow back in greater number when cut down to the ground, or 'coppiced'.

Adding to its unique personality are its spade-shaped leaves, its hanging catkins (decorating the bare winter branches like a chandelier) and, of course, its delicious nuts in the early autumn.

Hazel, with its straight rounds and softer wood, is a gift for many of the projects in this book, such as the stretch lantern (page 138), plant markers (page 35) and hedgerow basket (page 46). It's great for charcoal too (see page 74).

In ancient Rome, the hazel branch was considered a sign of peace. Cinderella planted a hazel rod to protect her mother's grave in the Grimm's fairy tale. The Celts associated hazel with wisdom and poetic inspiration – this is expressed beautifully in the tale of Fionn mac Cumhaill and the Salmon of Knowledge. Look it up!

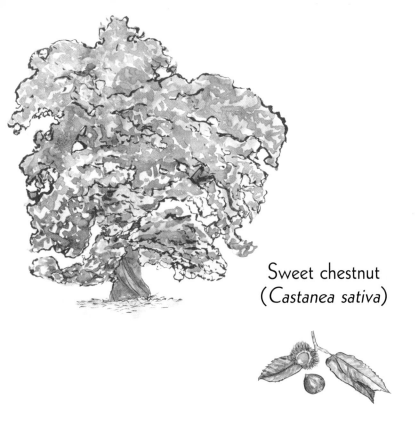

Sweet chestnut
(*Castanea sativa*)

With long, thin, serrated leaves and prickly pods containing its delicious edible fruit, the sweet chestnut is a majestic tree.

Traditionally used in the United Kingdom for making fences and roofing shingles, its wood is hard and durable and cleaves easily. Like ash, it is ring porous and so should not be used to make vessels or spoons. Chestnut bark is a wonderful material for weaving.

Chestnuts proliferated from Asia Minor across Europe; they owe some of this success to the travelling armies of Alexander the Great, who planted chestnut trees along the way so they would always have something to eat.

In this book, we use the bark of the sweet chestnut for the pot and knife sheath projects (page 56 and page 140). Let's have a quick look at the craft of stripping bark from trees.

BARK PREPARATION FOR WEAVING

Harvest bark in spring and early summer when the sap is rising. Harvesting must be undertaken carefully with supervision or training to allow regrowth and cause no lasting damage to the trees.

To remove the bark from a log or branch, run the tip of your knife along its length. Then using your fingers or a 'spud' (debarking tool), carefully peel the bark from the log.

When harvesting sweet chestnut, you need to scrape off the outer layer of the bark first before you peel the inner bark from the cambium (the magical part of the tree where the growth happens) using a blunt edge. This is because sweet chestnut bark is too brittle to work with when the outer bark is intact.

Willow bark can be used with the outer layer on or removed; using both provides a lovely colour contrast. For ash, cedar and other trees with thicker outer bark, the outer layer can be peeled apart from the inner layer after removal from the tree (splicing).

Once you have harvested a strip of bark, flatten the piece and roll it up in the opposite direction of the natural coil and hang to dry completely.

When you are ready to use the bark, you can soak it in cold water or run boiling water over it until it is supple. It can be cut into strips for weaving using a pair of scissors, a knife, a flint blade or a jerry leather stripper (a wonderful and heavy-duty tool designed for cutting leather into strips).

OUTER BARK
INNER BARK
CAMBIUM
WOOD

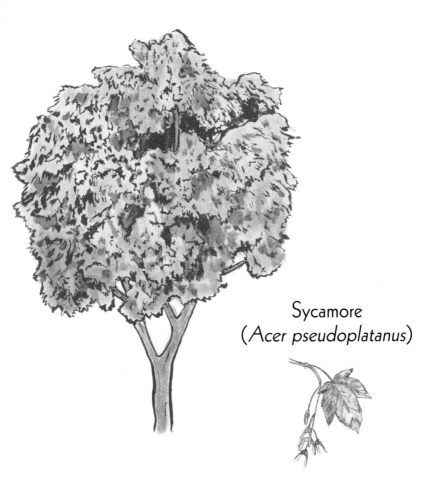

Sycamore
(*Acer pseudoplatanus*)

Growing large and dominant, the sycamore is hard to miss. Its winged fruit (samaras), which contain extremely fertile seeds, are sent out in every direction to propagate wherever they land. Throw in red-stalked leaves with a palmate shape typical of its family – the maple – and you have a tree full of character.

In Wales, sycamore was traditionally used to carve 'love spoons' – decorative objects presented to a sweetheart to show off the carver's skill. It's a lovely wood to carve and whittle and is ideal for making kitchenware as it has no taste.

Wild cherry
(*Prunus avium*)

Cherry is a handsome tree soaring upwards in straight trunks wrapped in bronze bark that peels off in rings. Cherry delivers new gifts every season: candyfloss blossom in the spring; hanging bunches of red cherries in summer; a fiery autumnal display of colour as the leaves turn and drop; and winter reveals its spreading branches and fine architecture.

Cherry can be harder to whittle and carve than other woods but is considerably easier the greener (fresher)

it is, and you will want to work with cherry when you see the attractive colours and grains within it. Cherry heartwood can range from golden-brown to salmon-pink and its sapwood is often creamy and paler. Other fruitwoods are similarly hard and beautifully coloured and definitely worth experimenting with!

The wild cherry is a mysterious tree in Scottish folklore: known as a 'witches' tree' in the north east, it was taboo to use its wood; while in the Highlands, to come across a cherry tree was auspicious.

White willow (*Salix alba*)

The beautiful and vast willow tree favours wet soil and is often found dipping its long, thin leaves and drooping branches into rivers and lakes. This link with water is mirrored in the folklore surrounding the great tree. The willow is also associated with mourning and fittingly has a profound connection to the underworld in Ancient Greek, Chinese and Japanese mythology.

Willow is soft for carving, though not durable enough for furniture or bigger projects. However, the flexible new growth on the branches ('rods' or 'whips') is perfect for weaving, particularly for some of the projects in this book (pages 46–49 and 60–62). As these rods require unique treatment, let's pause for a moment to examine the harvesting, storing and processing of willow for weaving overleaf.

Willow harvesting

Harvest your willow in the winter when the tree is dormant, the leaves have dropped and the sap is down. You will need a large knife or secateurs.

Storage

Sort your rods (also called 'whips') into 30cm-wide bundles by length (and by species, if you have harvested from other hedgerow trees too). Secure with string and allow to dry for at least six weeks so they can dehydrate and shrink.

Soaking

You can weave with green (fresh) or semi-green (left to dry for a few weeks) rods, but they may shrink further and compromise your finished project. When your rods have fully dried out they'll need to be rehydrated before you work with them. 'White' rods, with the bark stripped, can soak for just an hour or two and will be ready to work with. 'Brown' willow rods, with the bark on, tend to take around one day per 30cm to rehydrate. As with many of the materials in this book, the best way to learn about this is by trial, error and experimentation – so just have a go!

A helpful test to know your willow has soaked for long enough: take one rod and gently bend it at a right angle. If it splits, soak the bundle some more. If it feels slimy or the bark falls off, you may have over-soaked the willow. If so, you could try leaving it out for a couple of hours to see whether it mellows and becomes workable, or you could just start again with a new bundle. If it bends into a right angle, it is ready, so you can remove the bundle from the water and leave overnight to mellow.

Be aware that higher temperatures (whether inside or out) will affect the willow, causing it to dry out more quickly and become difficult to weave.

Splicing willow

One technique that will come in handy for the basket project (page 46) is splicing – splitting in half lengthways. Let's look at how to achieve that.

Carefully push the cutting edge of your knife 3cm into the butt (thicker end) of the rod and then twist the knife to open it up (figure 1). Now put the knife down and ease the two sides of the rod apart, moving your index finger down the rod to open it and using your thumb to add pressure on the side (figure 2).

If the split runs off to the side of the rod, you need to apply gentle force by pulling only on the thicker of the halves until the split has centralized. This is a tricky technique that will likely end in splits running off.

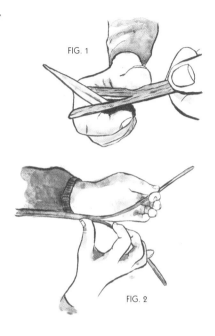

FIG. 1

FIG. 2

Other hedgerow species for weaving

Many common species found in gardens and hedgerows will also work well for weaving and bring their own distinct colour and personality. Some will need boiling to remove the bark, others require stripping of their thorns.

I invite you to read up on and experiment with other willow species, clematis, honeysuckle, ornamental dogwood and bramble, and any other flexible wood that catches your eye.

Tools

Some of the projects in this book require tools. I love working with hand tools in particular. This section will focus on tools and the techniques that work well with them.

A NOTE ON WORKING WITH CHILDREN AND TOOLS

Young people gain much from making things with their hands. For those who take the time to help children to safely develop their skills in this area, the social, physical, intellectual, emotional and spiritual benefits are clear to see. But remember, young people working with sharp tools should always be supervised by an adult and be encouraged to rest and take breaks.

Knife

In many ways, this is the most important tool you will own. Used for carving, whittling, stripping, scraping, cutting and maybe even spreading butter if you forget your cutlery, though do clean it first …

Please be vigilant and responsible about locking your tools away when they are not in use and do check local laws regarding the carrying of blades where you are.

SPLITTING
AXE

CARVING
AXE

Axes

Using an axe to shape, split and cut wood is one of life's great pleasures. You may choose to use a dedicated little carving axe, a big splitting axe or one that's a good all-rounder.

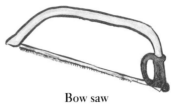

Bow saw

Bow saws are great for those bigger sawing jobs and can be used on your own or with a partner holding the other end. A bow saw can saw through any piece of wood narrower than the length of its blade.

Folding/pruning saw

A useful tool that I am rarely without when in the woods. It's great for sawing through anything up to the length of the blade, normally 15–25cm.

It can be useful to have a range of saws with different tooth sizes – use larger tooth sizes for more heavy-duty work such as making furniture and forestry and the finer sizes for gardening and woodworking.

Loppers

Like a big pair of scissors, loppers are great for cutting small twigs and branches up to around 3cm in diameter, depending on the model.

Secateurs

Useful for cutting twigs and small branches, secateurs also come in handy when making elder beads (page 68).

Froe

This L-shaped tool is used with a mallet to cleave wood along the grain. Hit the blade into the wood and then split it by twisting the handle. The froe can split any piece of wood that is narrower than its blade.

Shave horse

A shave horse is a combination of workbench and vice, used to hold a piece of wood in place with a foot-operated clamp. This allows the user to apply both arms and all their upper-body strength to the task.

Spoon or hook knife

These curved blades are built to carve the hollow cavity in spoons, bowls and other projects.

Multitool

A single tool containing a knife, file, screwdriver, pliers, wire cutter, bottle opener and more? Yes please!

Drawknife

Drawknives can be used for stripping bark or trimming and carving wood. The tool is held in two hands and pulled towards the body. It is best used with a shave horse.

While it is of course not a substitute for other tools, it is a very handy one to have around. Note that (although many people do) it is not recommended to whittle with a multitool or any other folding knife.

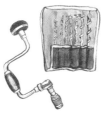

Bit and brace set

These hand-operated drills are used to bore holes into wood by applying pressure to the head while rotating the handle. Get hold of a drill bit set with a range from around 6–25mm. You can put a screwdriver bit in these drills, too. A very satisfying tool.

Electric drill

I love the feel of hand tools and don't use battery-powered or plug-in tools as much. However, an electric drill will come in handy for some of the projects in this book, such as the brush (page 50).

Scotch-eyed auger

This is another drilling tool and one that is particularly useful for bigger jobs. Slide a stick into the 'eye' at the top of the handle to create a T-bar handle. Then twist this and apply downward pressure to bore holes. I have various sizes from 1–5cm in diameter.

Sandpaper

Many carvers take pride in leaving their maker's marks visible on projects like the spoon (page 40). However, sandpaper is handy for refining the edges of the coat hook (page 54) and catapult (page 92). For a smooth finish, start with a coarse grit and progress to finer ones. I won't tell anyone if you sand your spoon too …

TOOL MAINTENANCE AND SHARPENING

A well-looked-after tool is a happy tool. Read up on how to care for each of them and the regular sharpening, cleaning, oiling and safe storage that will keep them in peak condition.

Knife techniques

Let's have a quick look at a few knife techniques you might use to make some of the projects in this book. I recommend you learn these skills under expert guidance, so have a look for local whittling and green woodworking courses. There are many helpful online tutorials too.

Free carving

This simple technique is for whittling projects. Sit in a comfortable and stable position. Hold the knife in the hand you write with and hold the wood in the other hand. Keep the cutting edge of your blade facing away from you and shave strips of wood, making long, sweeping cuts down the grain of the wood. This technique also works well if you use a chopping block for added support.

Batoning

This technique is for splitting or cleaving. Stand the wood vertically on a log or chopping block. Place the cutting edge of the knife on the end of the length of wood, positioning it at the point at which you would like it to enter. Use a mallet or stick to hit or tap the back of the knife, forcing the blade through the wood to split it along the grain. Use this technique with an axe, billhook or froe for larger projects.

Stop cut

Apply downward pressure with your knife while carefully rolling the knife to make a vertical cut. Often used with the thumb push stroke to make a notch.

Thumb push stroke

Gain greater control over small or awkward cuts by pushing the back of the blade with the thumb of your helping hand (the one not holding the knife).

Pull stroke

This technique is just like peeling an apple. Use the thumb of your knife hand to steady the wood while supporting it with your helping hand. Then carefully draw the knife towards yourself, taking care to keep your thumb out of the path of the blade. You may wish to wear a thumb guard for protection.

Chest lever grip

This technique looks dangerous but is very controlled when used properly. Turn the knife around in your hand, stick your elbows out and bring the wood and knife into your chest with your thumbs on top and cutting edge facing away from you. Bring your elbows into your body as you cut – this allows you to use your chest and shoulder muscles to take more wood off with each stroke.

Cordage and useful knots

Some knowledge of knots will help you with many of the
projects in this book. Let's look first at different types of cordage
you might use for practical and creative purposes and then
turn to the knot techniques.

Types of cordage

Rope

Climbing rope

I like a strong and soft rope and usually
use hempex (polyhemp) – a synthetic,
three-strand twisted rope made out
of polypropylene fibres, normally
between 16–24mm thick.

For hammocks (page 122) and netting,
I use cotton braided rope as it is soft
and ties well.

For projects such as the rope swing
(page 94) or the zip line (page 96),
where there is a risk of falling from
a height if the rope fails, it's really
important that we can trust the rope.
For this reason, I recommend rope
graded for climbing use. I favour a
static (not stretchy) rope around
11 or 12mm thick.

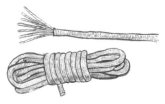

Paracord

Paracord was developed by the US military during the Second World War as 'parachute cord' and today is used across the world and even in space – in 1997 NASA astronauts used paracord to repair damaged insulation on the Hubble Space Telescope!

It is strong (Type III or '550 paracord' can hold up to 250kg/550lbs of static weight), soft and mould-resistant, making it ideal for use in the outdoors.

The thin inner strands can be removed for jobs where a smaller strand will come in handy, such as tying off your catapult (page 92).

Sisal

A stiff and strong fibre derived from the agave plant of the same name. Sisal is available in many thicknesses, from thin strings to thick ropes. I use a lot of it, normally around 3mm thick, for structures and crafts.

Jute

Jute is a strong, glossy fibre that comes from two plants in the linden family that are thought to originate from South Asia. I normally use the thin and soft 2mm 'gardening twine' form that comes in earthy brown as well as other colours. Jute works well for crafts and non-weight-bearing projects.

Yarn

Traditionally used for knitting or making cloth, yarn can be made of natural or synthetic fibres and works really well for projects such as the 'god's eye' weaving (page 65) and dreamcatcher (page 84). Use a biodegradable natural yarn, especially if you're planning to work outdoors. You could also experiment with colouring your yarn using natural dyes by boiling it with roots, berries, beans, barks, leaves and wood.

Knots

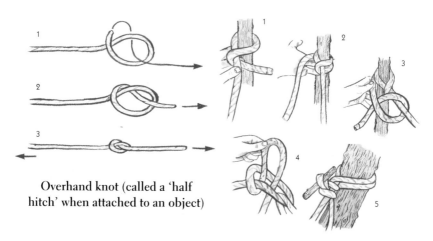

Overhand knot (called a 'half hitch' when attached to an object)

Quick release tension knot

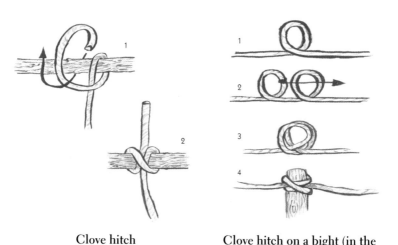

Clove hitch

Clove hitch on a bight (in the middle of the line)

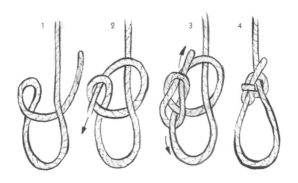

Running bowline

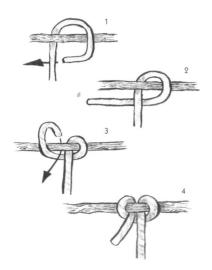

Lark's foot knot

Lark's foot (on the bight)

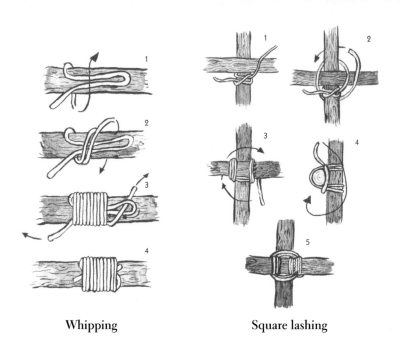

Whipping

Square lashing

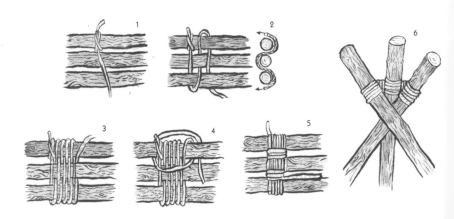

Tripod lashing

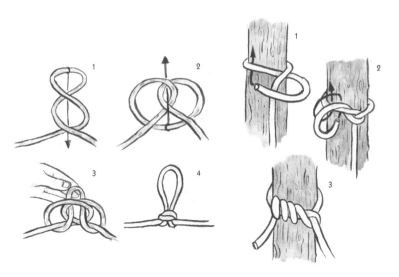

Alpine butterfly knot

Timber hitch

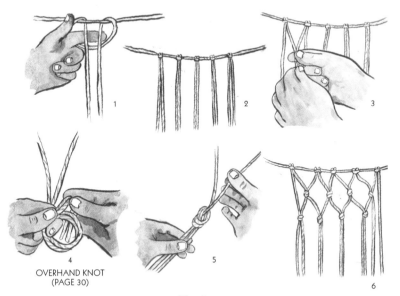

OVERHAND KNOT
(PAGE 30)

Netting

33

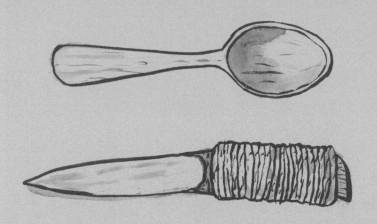

Home sticks

Furnish your home with practical and beautiful stick-based
projects, from a spoon to a broom – each as individual as
the tree from which it came and a wonderfully sustainable
alternative to shop-bought products.

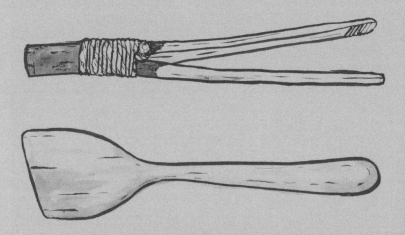

Plant markers

Label the plants in your garden with these lovely markers; they are useful, easy to make and look great.

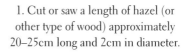

1. Cut or saw a length of hazel (or other type of wood) approximately 20–25cm long and 2cm in diameter.

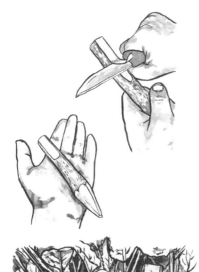

2. At one end of the stick, whittle a flat surface around 8–10cm long on two opposite sides of the wood.

3. Carve the other end to a point.

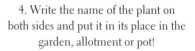

4. Write the name of the plant on both sides and put it in its place in the garden, allotment or pot!

2

Knife

It's a lovely thing, using a knife to make
… a knife! This is a great whittling project
and a delightful way to spend your time –
sitting under a tree creating piles of wood
shavings all around you.

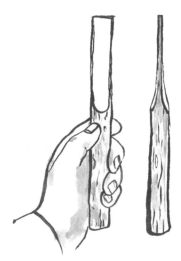

1. Find a straight length of green
(fresh) wood 20–25cm in length and as
wide in diameter as you would like the
handle of your knife.

Starting halfway along, use your knife
to shave wood off on both sides until
the top half of the stick is flat and at
least 3mm thick.

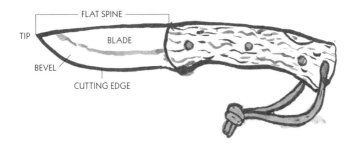

FLAT SPINE

TIP

BLADE

BEVEL

CUTTING EDGE

2. The neat thing about the next stage – shaping the blade – is you have a model of the item you are trying to create in your other hand!

Look at the knife, notice its features and use your blade to create the flat spine, bevel and cutting edge, and the tapering on both sides to the tip.

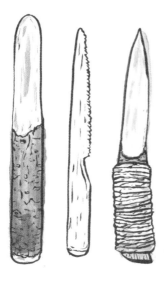

3. Leave to dry and rub some natural oil (poppy, hemp, linseed or other) into your creation to finish and preserve it.

Your creation may become a decorative object with carvings on the handle. It could feature a serrated blade, become a more rounded butter knife or even a letter opener.

You could also use whipping (page 32) to make a handle for your whittled knife.

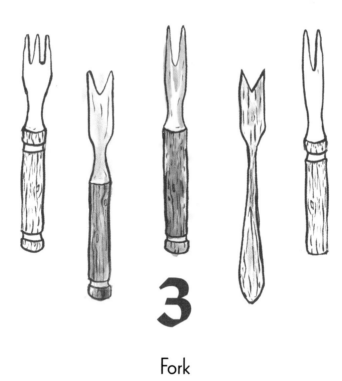

Fork

Stuck without a fork on a campout? Or maybe you're just looking for another reason to whittle the afternoon away? These forks are as enjoyable to make as they are to use. You can make yours with two, three or even four prongs.

They work particularly well for toasting as the handles won't heat up in the way metal handles would – but don't leave them in the fire for too long as they will burn!

As always, experiment and play with different woods but do be careful to read up on your local species to avoid toxic woods.

1. This one starts in the same way as the knife project (page 36). Find a length of green (fresh), straight-grained wood around 20–40cm in length, depending on how long you want your fork to be. The width of the wood will set the size of your handle, so check it sits nicely in your hand.

2. Starting at the point at which your handle will end, use your knife to shave wood off on either side until the fork head is flat and at least 3mm thick, tapering the end to a flat screwdriver-style point.

3. Create the prongs by carving out a V-shape from the fork head. To do this, use a pencil to mark out the V-shape. Then turn the blade around and use the tip of the knife to cut up towards the ends of the fork prongs. Alternatively you could use a saw: make a straight cut into the fork head in the space between each prong, then use the tip of the knife to widen it to your liking.

4. Take some time to decorate your handle and perhaps thin out the stem of the fork between the handle and prongs. Smooth your fork with long strokes of the blade (or even sandpaper), leave to dry and rub some natural oil into your creation to finish and preserve it.

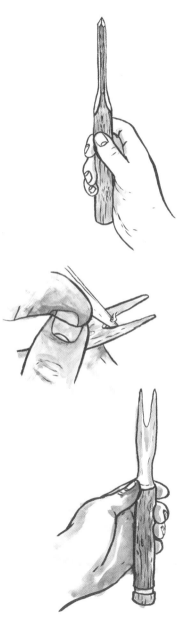

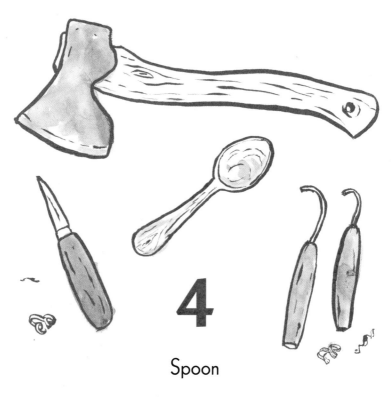

4

Spoon

Carving a spoon is a slow, satisfying process that serves as an antidote to this busy modern world. It's a real skill and takes time to cultivate, but it's worth it.

Experiment with softer materials like birch and look for straight, knot-free wood to start with. Then you can move on to more challenging materials like cherry wood, which is harder to carve and beautifully salmon-coloured. A knotty piece of wood will be trickier to work with but will have its own natural and unique character. Again, please be careful and read up on your local species to avoid toxic woods if you plan to use your spoon for food preparation.

1. First, you need to make a 'blank' – a flat, rectangular piece of wood from which you'll carve your spoon. You could do this by quartering a large log, as with the spatula (page 44), or by simply splitting a smaller round in half, as shown here.

The length of the log or round you will need is set by the size of spoon you wish to make.

2. Draw the shape of your spoon on the blank and use an axe to roughly shape it. It's getting there!

3. Now it's time to sit down, relax and begin the slow and meditative process of shaping and smoothing the handle and head. Make long strokes with a whittling knife along the grain. Scoop out the 'bowl' with a curved spoon knife – start with a tiny indent, gradually deepening it with shavings across the grain. Take your time over this and have plenty of rest breaks!

4. When you're done, allow your spoon to dry slowly somewhere cool to prevent cracking. Rub a natural oil (walnut, hemp, linseed or other) into your spoon to preserve and finish.

5

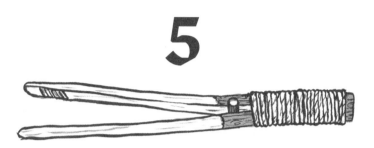

Tongs

You will love making these tongs. Try mini ones for smaller hands too – or even tiny 'tweezers'! Hazel works well, but you can play and experiment with different woods. Remember to read up on your local species to avoid toxic woods if you plan to use your tongs for food preparation.

1. Cut a length of green (fresh) wood around 30cm long and 2–4cm in diameter. Stand it up on a log or chopping block and use the batoning technique (page 26) to tap the knife blade halfway down the wood. Make your cut slightly off-centre so that one side of the finished tongs is thinner than the other and bends nicely for picking things up.

2. Slide a small stick two-thirds of the way down into the cut you have made to open it up. Don't let the two pieces split apart completely!

3. Use whipping (page 32) to make a handle with sisal or paracord. This makes a cool grip but also stops the tongs splitting in half.

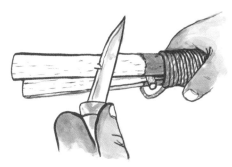

4. Now finish the tongs by stripping the bark and smoothing the edges. You may also want to carve serrated teeth into the inside of each prong for extra grip.

6

Spatula

We don't ordinarily give much thought to the humble spatula, but think about how useful it is – mixing, lifting and flipping our food every day at home or in the wild!

It's also a nice-and-simple green woodworking project for you to enjoy. Birch and maple work well; fruitwoods are harder to carve but are also lovely. Make sure you read up on your local species to avoid toxic woods if you plan to use your spatula for food preparation.

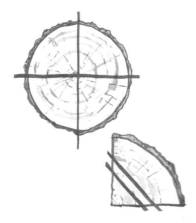

1. Find a round of green (fresh) wood around 20–30cm long and 12cm in diameter. Use an axe or a froe to divide it into quarters. Cleave (split) a thin, rectangular piece from one of the quarters, avoiding the pithy centre of the log, to make your 'blank'. The blank should be as close to 4mm thick as possible and 5–8cm wide.

If you need to thin your blank further, it's easier to use a drawknife and shave horse (page 24).

2. Draw a spatula shape on the blank with a pencil or even a piece of charcoal from the fire. It's helpful to draw a line down the centre from end to end to keep your spatula symmetrical. If your wood has any knots, it's best to position these in the handle of the spatula rather than the 'spoon'.

3. Use a knife (or an axe if you have more wood to take off) to shape the blank into a rough spatula shape, moving closer to the pencil line.

4. Working carefully, use a whittling knife to bring a more refined shape to the spatula. (A drawknife and shave horse would also be ideal for this task.) First, shape the profile, then the head and finally the flat faces of the spatula. Think about forming a thinned tip at the end and a comfortable handle. You may also wish to smooth the spatula with sandpaper and treat the wood using a natural oil such as linseed or hemp.

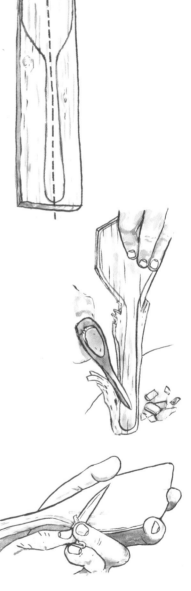

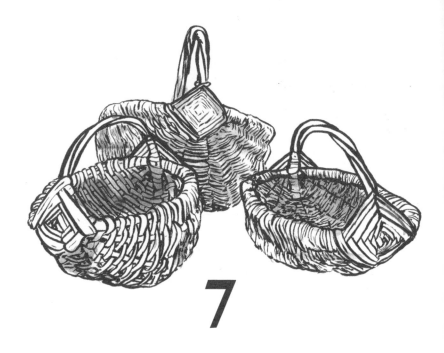

7

Hedgerow basket

Weaving is a craft that puts us in touch with something very ancient within ourselves, although it was not that long ago that there was a weaver in every village who would have made all manner of household items in this enchanting way.

This 'hoop frame' basket design can be made using a number of species commonly found in hedgerows, such as willow, clematis, honeysuckle and bramble (see pages 20–21 for more information on collection and preparation). I learnt a lot of the weaving skills and techniques you'll find in this book from the amazing Mollie and Nick McMillen, who work in the south-west of England.

1. Take four rods of willow, each around 2m long and approximately 1cm wide at the butt (thicker end), and make two hoops. For more guidance, see steps 1–3 of the wreath project (page 78).

Fit the hoops inside each other to set the depth of your basket – the lower the position of the horizontal hoop, the shallower the basket (and vice versa). Make sure the rod butts on the handle hoop are lower than the basket rim.

Tie the hoops in place with pipe cleaners or string. You can remove these during step 2. It's also a good idea to tie a piece of string to your handle to remind yourself which way up the structure goes! This can be taken off after step 3.

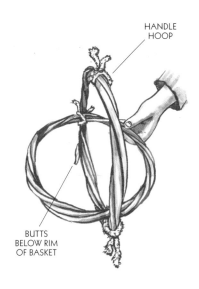

HANDLE HOOP

BUTTS BELOW RIM OF BASKET

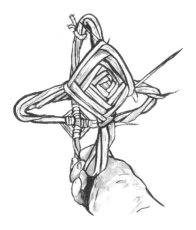

2. It's time to fasten the hoops together permanently. You will need two more willow rods, each at least 1.2m long. Splice the rods (page 21) to leave you with four half-rods.

At this point, use the 'god's eye' weave, featured on pages 65–67, to fasten the hoops together using two spliced half-rods on each side. Trim the loose ends.

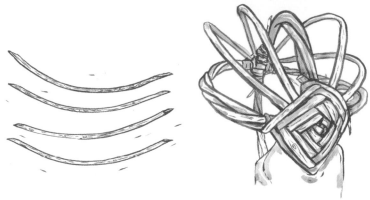

3. Now we will make the 'ribs' that create the framework for the basket. Cut four lengths of hazel or older, drier willow. 'Slype' (cleanly cut at an angle) the ends so that they bend and sit snugly into the back of the 'god's eye' fastening on each side.

Play with the lengths of the ribs, cutting a bit more off each time until you have the profile you desire.

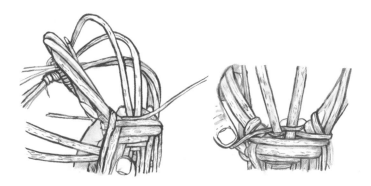

4. Let's get weaving! Gather a bundle of willow or other hedgerow rods – each rod should be at least 1.2m long. Begin with the tip (thinner end) of a long, thin rod and weave in and out of the ribs, over and under, starting out at the side of the basket and working towards the centre.

Note: If your rod finishes on a butt, begin the next weave with a butt (and vice versa with the tips). Make sure the protruding ends stay on the inside of the structure and sit next to the ribs rather than the basket rim.

You may also choose to add more ribs as you go to ensure a smoother curve at the base of your basket.

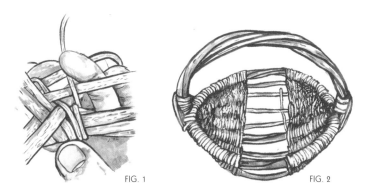

FIG. 1   FIG. 2

5. Continue your weaving, adding more rods and alternating the weave over and under the ribs with each adjacent rod. Swap ends from time to time as your weave moves towards the centre.

It is good to 'double wrap' your rods at the rim (go twice around) on either side at the start of your weaves (figure 1) until they are in two straight parallel lines heading towards the centre, as shown in figure 2.

Simply carry on working until the weave meets in the centre and your hedgerow basket is ready!

8

Brush

You are going to love this one. Two sticks, some coconut fibres (or similar), a bit of glue … and you've made your own brush! Use yours for cleaning, clearing or even painting. Or simply admire it. It's a rustic thing of beauty.

It's helpful to have a bench vice to hold your pieces in place while you work. Also, this is one of the few projects in this book where we will use electric tools, specifically an electric drill, but you can, of course, use hand tools instead.

1. Begin with two rounds of green (fresh) wood. The handle should be 1.6–2cm in diameter and 14cm long. The head should be 3–4cm in diameter and 12–13cm long. See pages 20-21 for more information on collection and preparation of materials.

2. Use a 15-mm bit to drill 15mm into the centre of the brush head. Whittle down one end of the handle until it is just too big for the hole. Secure the brush head in a vice, if possible, and use a mallet to force the tapered end of the handle into the hole so it sits nice and tight. At this point, use some sandpaper to smooth the ends and edges of your brush.

3. Next, let's drill the holes for the bristles. Turn the brush head over 180 degrees and use a 15-mm Forstner bit to drill 15mm into the midpoint of the head. Drill an identical hole on either side, each angled slightly away from the central hole to allow the bristles to splay.

4. Measure out three 15-mm bundles of coconut fibres or similar. Tie with rubber bands (as shown) and trim at each end until they are roughly 15cm long. Check that one end of each bundle fits inside a hole on the brush head before fixing them in place with epoxy resin glue. Leave to dry for 24 hours. Then remove the rubber bands and trim the brush ends to your desired length.

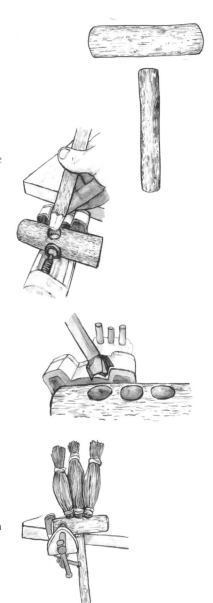

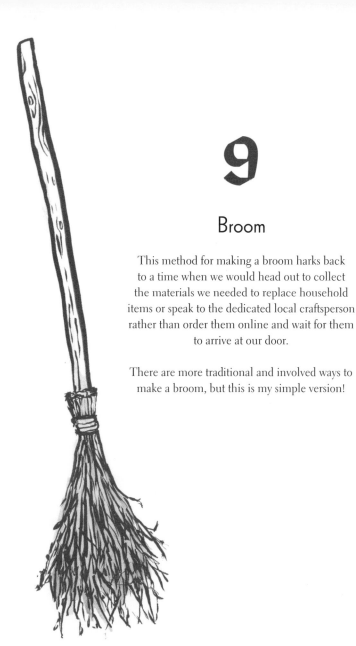

9

Broom

This method for making a broom harks back
to a time when we would head out to collect
the materials we needed to replace household
items or speak to the dedicated local craftsperson
rather than order them online and wait for them
to arrive at our door.

There are more traditional and involved ways to
make a broom, but this is my simple version!

1. Collect a bundle of birch twigs – it should be big enough for you to need two hands to hold it at its widest point. In an ideal world, you would leave the bundle to season (dry) for a few months or even a year as this lengthens the lifespan of your broom, but don't worry if you don't have time for this!

2. Fasten your bundle tightly together using string, wire or natural cordage and trim the ends of the twigs around 5–10cm from the fastening.

3. Find your broom handle; any straight-ish length will work. (As a rule of thumb, around 1.2m will suit an average adult, but choose a length that's comfortable for your height.) Whittle one end of your handle to a rough point.

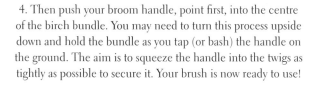

4. Then push your broom handle, point first, into the centre of the birch bundle. You may need to turn this process upside down and hold the bundle as you tap (or bash) the handle on the ground. The aim is to squeeze the handle into the twigs as tightly as possible to secure it. Your brush is now ready to use!

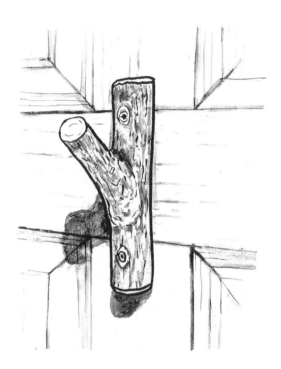

10

Coat hook

These coat hooks are wonderful – each one as charmingly unique as the trees from which they came. As well as harnessing nature's beauty, the magic of these hooks is that the design takes advantage of the immense strength of the point at which a branch meets the tree.

1. Go and gather your wood. Search for thicker branches with protruding thinner branches – one fallen tree or large bough could provide many of these!

Cut pieces around 8–15cm in length and more than 2cm in diameter (at the thickest point).

2. Fix one of the pieces in a vice and use a medium-toothed folding saw to cut along the grain and through the wood vertically; this will form the straight, flat back that will sit snugly against the wall or door.

3. Sand the back of the hook and all its ends and edges. Start with a coarse grit before moving to a finer one.

4. Drill a hole above and below the arm of the hook – the holes should be slightly smaller than the screws you plan to use to fix it to the wall or door. It's also a good idea to countersink (make a conical cut where the screw head will sit) using an electric drill or the tip of your whittling knife. Your hook is now ready to be screwed to the wall!

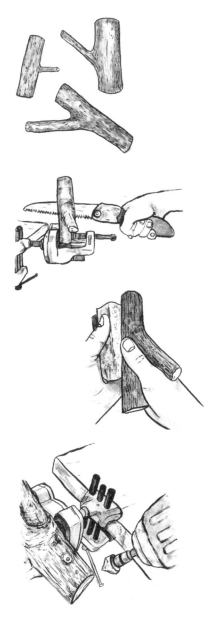

11

Bark pots

These pots are so satisfying to make; the results are wonderful. And you will love working with the soft strips of sweet chestnut bark (page 16). You could also use cedar, birch, elm or willow bark, or leaves from plants such as iris and cattails.

You can make lots of shapes and sizes (like the ones below). Simply experiment with different combinations of strips for the lattice in step 1, always using an even number of strips to weave vertically and horizontally.

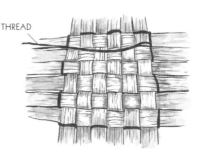

THREAD

1. Let's start with 12 strips of bark, each one 33cm long and 1.2cm wide. Place them flat and work them in and out of each other in a 'chequerboard' weave, starting in the middle and working outwards. Begin with two strips, adding more as you go and using a ruler to ensure the weave stays central.

2. Once you have worked six strips vertically and horizontally into the 'chequerboard' weave, you will have a central square. Take some fine thread and tie it off on one corner. Then weave the thread around the square and tie it off where you started. This will help to secure the base of the pot.

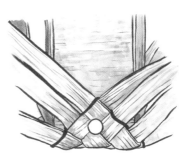

3. Place a wooden block diagonally in the centre of the square lattice. This design requires a block measuring 5.8 x 5.8 x 11cm. Secure the block on the underside with drawing pins. Then fold each side up and pin in place.

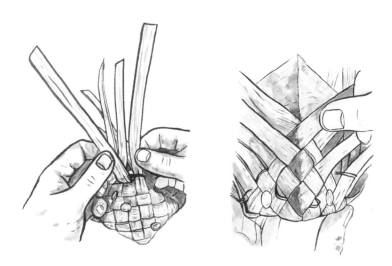

4. Let's begin to weave the sides of the pot. Starting at the base of each corner, weave each strip under and over the strips they meet as they fold diagonally upwards at a 45-degree angle.

Rotate from corner to corner as your weave progresses. You can cut and remove the thread, pull out the pins and slide out the block when you have woven at least 3cm along each side.

FIG. 1

5. Continue until you have reached your desired height or there
is only 5cm of strip left to work with at the top.

Arrange the protruding bark so all the strips that point to the
right are on the outside of the weave. Cut the ends to a point
and fold down to the right at a 45-degree angle. This should give
you a flat 'top' and align the folded strips with the weave of the
basket. Then tuck the strips into the weave (figure 1).

Carefully snip the ends off above and below the rim (figure 2)
and your pot is finished!

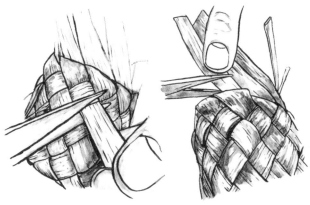

FIG. 2

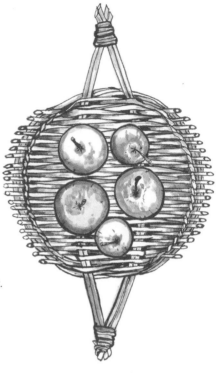

12

Catalan platter

Serve bread or fruit on this charming platter; a beautiful object in its own right.

As the name suggests, this design originates from Catalunya; it's a place that is very close to my heart and the land where I developed many of the skills featured in this book.

1. Begin by making one 30cm hoop from two 2m rods of willow using the same technique shown in steps 1–3 of the wreath project (page 78).

Then take four straight rods at least 70cm in length. Fasten the rods to the hoop in pairs using string or pipe cleaners, leaving equal space between the rods and the sides of the hoop. The rods will later form the platter's handles.

2. Now let's weave the base of the platter. Use rods of willow, dogwood or hazel. Each rod should be 10cm longer than the diameter of your hoop (40cm in this case). Starting at the centre, work the base rods under and over the handle rods and outer hoop, alternating the pattern from row to row.

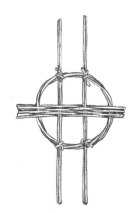

After weaving 6–8 rods, remove the string or pipe cleaners – this will allow you to move the rods as necessary as you continue weaving to fill the hoop.

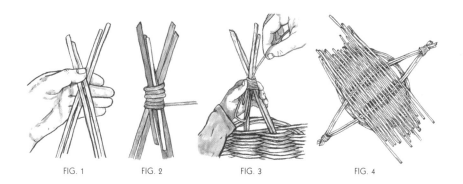

FIG. 1   FIG. 2   FIG. 3   FIG. 4

3. It's time to tie the handle ends together. Cross the rods right over left (figure 1). Take a thin, flexible willow rod, around 0.9–1.2m in length, and wrap it three times around the join; note that I have tucked an extra stick in place here (figure 2). Slide the stick out after wrapping the rod around the join and tuck the thin end of the rod into the space left by the stick. Then pull tight and trim both ends of the rod (figure 3). Repeat to secure the other handle end (figure 4).

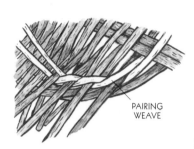

PAIRING
WEAVE

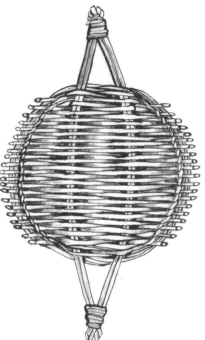

4. Let's add a pairing weave for extra strength and decorative flair (although you could stop here and snip the ends around the platter if you are happy with the design).

Grab four 0.9–1.2m rods of flexible willow – you'll use two for each side. Work two into the weave just inside the rim of the platter, and weave around the edge, always taking the left-hand rod over the other rod, behind the basket weave and to the front again. Repeat this with each rod alternately all the way around, using two rods on each side. Then simply snip the ends around the platter and you are done!

13

Pencil pot

A simple and pleasing design, these look lovely around the house or woodland camp.

1. Cut a round of wood that is the same size as you would like your pot. The example on this page is 10cm long and 8cm in diameter.

Choose wood with an attractive bark pattern such as cherry or birch.

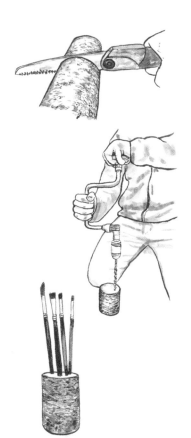

2. Drill holes into the end of the round for your pencils. A standard pencil is 7mm in diameter, so an 8-mm drill bit should do.

For this, you could use a bit and brace set (page 25) or, of course, an electric drill. You may need to clamp the wood to keep it in place while drilling.

You don't have to use the pot for pencils. How about filling it with paintbrushes, toothbrushes or even candles? You may need to drill bigger holes depending on your intended use.

Stick craft

Get crafty with these projects to create beautiful and
decorative objects. Witness the magic that happens when we
apply creativity and experimentation to the humble stick.

14

God's eye weaving

Weaving is a calming and meditative process that results in a beautifully crafted object that will last for years. These *Ojo de Dios* or 'god's eye' weavings are just lovely.

It is important to recognize that these are spiritual and votive objects for many people in northern Mexico. I present this technique with respect and gratitude and urge you to read more about the culture and practices of these Indigenous communities.

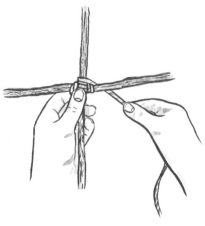

1. Use square lashing (page 32) or a rubber band to tie two sticks together at a right angle.

2. Attach coloured yarn to one stick at the centre using a double overhand knot (page 30).

Pull the yarn and wrap it one full loop around the adjacent stick before moving on to the next one. Carry on, being careful to move in the same direction and wrap it in the same way each time.

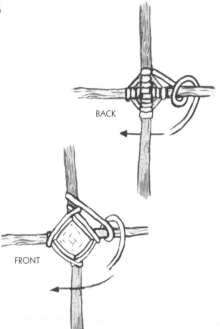

BACK

FRONT

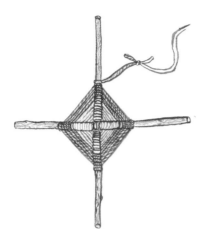

3. Your weaving will grow and move away from the centre with each rotation.

To change colour, simply tie the end of the yarn to the new colour and continue, pushing any loose ends to the back. Carry on until you are happy with your design. Add a loop for hanging your weaving and maybe even some tassels.

4. You can also experiment with three sticks rather than two, play with leaving spaces between the weaving, and try multiple pieces of string for a more complex design. The results are spectacular.

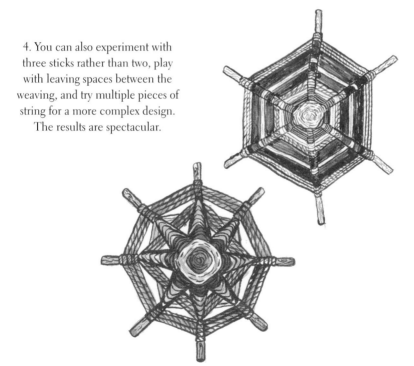

15

Elder jewellery

The beauty of elder (page 12) is the soft pith inside the wood and the many possibilities for creativity this provides. I'll be sharing some elder projects with you over the following pages, starting with this simple classic – elder beads and jewellery.

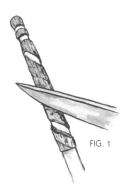

FIG. 1

FIG. 2

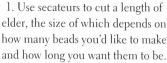

1. Use secateurs to cut a length of elder, the size of which depends on how many beads you'd like to make and how long you want them to be.

Score lines into the bark (figure 1) before using the knife to tease the strips off (figure 2). Try hoops, spirals or any pattern you choose!

It's easier to create the designs now rather than when you have cut the length into smaller sections.

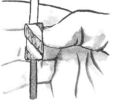

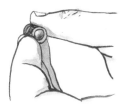

2. Cut the length into beads and use a straight stick or tent peg to push out the soft pith in the centre. Thread your beads onto the cordage you'll use for your jewellery before tying off with a double overhand knot (page 30).

You can make bracelets, necklaces, headdresses and all kinds of decorations using this simple technique. Try experimenting with other species such as willow for green beads or ornamental dogwood for beautiful red ones.

Elder whistle

This one takes a bit of practice to get right and therein lies the pleasure. Lose yourself in the making process and then enjoy the reward of that sweet, shrill whistle at the end.

Similar designs made of sheep bone dating back to the Iron Age have been found in the UK. It's an ancient and noisy tradition!

1. Cut a length of elder around 10–12cm long and use a straight stick or tent peg to push out the soft pith – remove about 8cm but don't remove the pith all the way through. Clear the cavity in the centre as cleanly as you can.

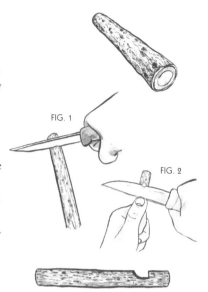

FIG. 1

FIG. 2

2. Make a stop cut around 2cm from the end without pith (figure 1). Then use a thumb push stroke (figure 2) to create a clean and curved cut on the top of the whistle (figure 3) around 2cm in length. See page 27 for more details on these cutting techniques.

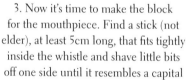

FIG. 3

3. Now it's time to make the block for the mouthpiece. Find a stick (not elder), at least 5cm long, that fits tightly inside the whistle and shave little bits off one side until it resembles a capital 'D' (as shown). Push this into the mouthpiece and trim until the block sits flush with the end of the whistle; this will create the all-important stream of air against a sharp edge that results in a high-pitched whistle.

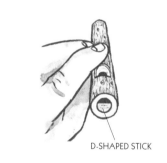

D-SHAPED STICK

4. Finally, shave to create a curved underside at the bottom of the mouthpiece and get whistling!

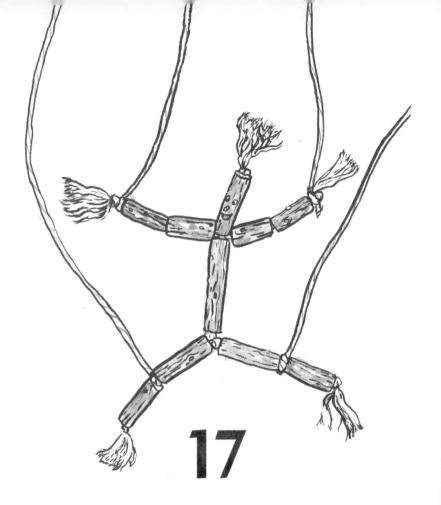

17

Puppet

This is a wonderful design; it was taught to me by my mentor, woodsman Patrick Harrison. Why not try it and then have a go at making bigger ones, animals or fantastic creatures?

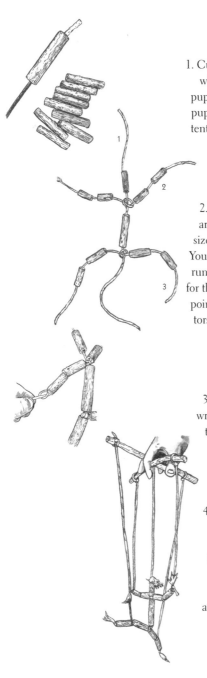

1. Cut ten lengths of elder wood. These pieces will form the different body parts of your puppet; the longer the pieces, the bigger the puppet and vice versa. Use a straight stick or tent peg to push out the soft pith and hollow out the elder lengths.

2. Decide which pieces will be the head, arms, legs and torso and cut the pieces to size. You can use the illustration as a guide. You'll need three pieces of string for this: one running through the head and torso (1), one for the arms (2) and one for the legs (3). At the point where the arm and leg strings meet the torso string, tie an overhand knot (page 30).

3. Tie an overhand knot at your puppet's wrists, ankles and head and fray the ends of the string to create hands, feet and hair.

4. Finally, tie longer cords to your puppet's knees and wrists and get that puppet moving! You may wish to use square lashing (page 32) and two sticks to create a wooden cross to control the puppet, or you could share the strings with friends and work together to gain greater control of your puppet's movements.

18

Charcoal pencils

Make your own woodland pencils with this multi-step, multi-skill and multi-material project! This is a great activity to do when you've got a fire going and are feeling creative.

1. Fill a metal biscuit tin with thin sticks – stripped hazel and willow work well. It's a good use for your offcuts from weaving projects such as the hedgerow basket and Catalan platter (pages 46 and 60). Punch a hole in the lid with a pointed tent peg. Then put the lid back on and place the tin in the fire.

When smoke stops coming out of the hole, carefully remove the tin from the fire. Plug the hole in the lid with the tent peg and leave the tin to cool in a safe place.

2. Cut lengths of elder and whittle the ends to a pencil-like 'point'. Use a tent peg or stick to push out the spongy pith and create a hollow centre into which you can push a charcoal stick. Time to get drawing!

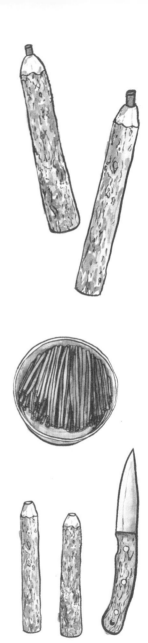

19

Paintbrushes

Experiment with natural materials to make your own paintbrushes. Each one will have its own unique character, feel and, in some cases, even smell! Painting with rosemary sprigs and enjoying the aromas released as you create is a magical multi-sensory pleasure.

Instead of shop-bought paint, you could use natural dyes such as turmeric and beetroot, or even just good old-fashioned mud.

1. Head out and look for sticks and 'brushes' – search for materials that will have interesting textures … feathers, herbs and seed heads are all lovely and there are so many other options.

Do consider the ecological impact of your foraging (page 7).

2. Use string or biodegradable rubber bands to attach the brush materials to your sticks and get painting!

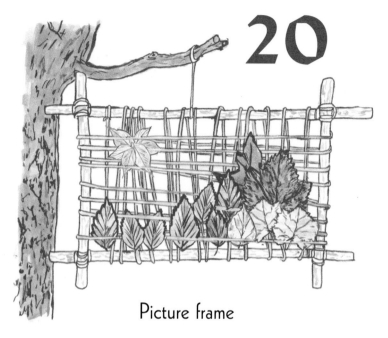

Picture frame

Making these picture frames is such a joy – and that's before
you've even added materials to create your art. Have fun!

1. Find four sticks and lay them on
the ground to decide the size of your
frame. Once you're happy, square lash
(page 32) the frame at each corner.

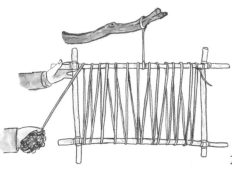

2. Hang the frame from a tree branch with some string. Loop coloured yarn (or similar) vertically around the top and bottom of the frame. Then weave horizontally from side to side to create a lattice effect.

3. Collect natural materials and tuck them into the weave to create a literal or abstract image. Satisfyingly, as you add more materials and your picture becomes more striking, the weave will become tighter and tighter. Time to get creating!

21

Wreath

These wreaths are simple and beautiful. They can also be embellished with sprigs, seeds, flowers and berries. And they are not just for Christmas – decorate them with seasonal items all year round to celebrate the Earth and her cycles. A spring, summer or autumn wreath is a special thing indeed.

We'll use about eight willow rods, each at least 2m long, to make a wreath around 25–30cm in diameter. See page 20 for more information on the collection and storage of weaving materials.

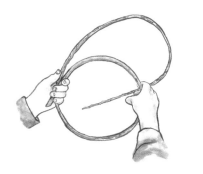

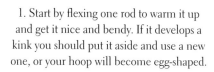

1. Start by flexing one rod to warm it up and get it nice and bendy. If it develops a kink you should put it aside and use a new one, or your hoop will become egg-shaped.

Hold the butt (thicker end) in your hand and shape the rod into a hoop before guiding it into the circle, like an overhand knot (page 30).

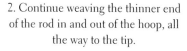

2. Continue weaving the thinner end of the rod in and out of the hoop, all the way to the tip.

3. Add a second rod, positioning the butt on the opposite side of the wreath (as shown). Repeat the same process, weaving the rod around the hoop to the tip.

(If you are making a hedgerow basket or Catalan platter, stop here, trim the butts and tips and turn back to page 47 or 60.)

4. Continue to add more rods, spacing the butts evenly around the circle to keep it nice and balanced in shape. Eight rods should be enough but you can keep going until you are happy with its volume. Then neatly trim any bits that are protruding.

22

Tiny furniture

I just love making these little tables and chairs. There is something so meditative and calming about working on a small scale. I always find myself getting carried away making tiny plates, cups and bottles.

You can also scale these up and make them human-sized too, or at least big enough for the kids!

Table

1. Find (or cut) a length of knot-free, green (fresh) wood of around 7cm in length and 9cm in diameter. Use a saw to make a 2–3cm stop cut (page 27) in the wood on all sides, around 3cm from one end.

2. Use the batoning technique (page 26) to gently cleave away the wood up to the stop cut. Repeat all the way around until you have created a pedestal leg.

3. Flip it over and your tiny table is done! Now let's make some chairs …

Chairs

1. Find (or cut) a length of knot-free, green (fresh) wood of around 12cm in length and 6cm in diameter. Saw a stop cut 3–4cm into one side, around 3cm from one end.

2. Use the batoning technique to split the wood away up to the stop cut. Repeat steps 1–2 to make more chairs.

Now put it all together and dress the table (and yourself) for a fairy tea party!

Mobile

Use natural materials to make a mobile to hang in the garden or around the home.

1. Find one or more sticks. You may choose to carve designs into them or decorate them with paint and natural dyes. (For a few ideas, see page 69.)

2. Collect the natural treasures that will hang from the mobile. Remember to only gather what is abundant and only take what you need. Poppy seed heads, pine cones, feathers and other delights will work well. Take your time and enjoy this process.

3. Tie your treasures to your mobile using coloured yarn if you are feeling bright and colourful.

You could also square lash (page 32) multiple sticks together to make a 3D structure for your mobile.

24

Dreamcatcher

Try making a beautiful and decorative dreamcatcher. Placed above the bed, they are said to protect those who sleep below.

I present this project with thanks to the great and old Indigenous cultures of North America, to whom this tradition belongs. Though the new form bears little resemblance to the original, it is intended as a respectful homage rather than an appropriation.

The version on these pages is a funky and imperfect woodland take on the dreamcatcher. Alternatively you can use steps 1–3 of the wreath project (page 79) to make a longer-lasting and rounder hoop.

1. Find a young, bendy willow or hazel branch and strip the leaves. Now curve and roughly twist it into an imperfect hoop, weaving the thinner end of the branch in and out of the hoop, all the way to the tip (see left).

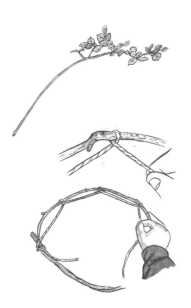

2. Take a long piece of string or coloured yarn. Tie one end onto the hoop to secure the join. Pull your string 5–10cm along, wrap it around the hoop and back through the opening before pulling it nice and tight. Repeat this process all the way around the hoop to create the framework for your net.

3. Continue by looping the string around the midpoint of each length of string (as shown). The more precise you are about finding the midpoint, the more perfect the net will be. This one is lovely and imperfect!

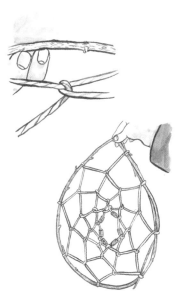

4. As you work your way into the centre, why not add elder beads (page 68) or change the colour of your string or yarn? Once you reach the centre, secure the end of the string with a double overhand knot (page 30) and trim away the excess string. Then collect feathers and other natural items to hang from the bottom of your beautiful dreamcatcher.

25

Nests

We see bird's nests in trees, pylons and on cliffs but may not give much thought to the extraordinary craft involved in their construction. Have you ever tried making one?

In doing so, we really appreciate the extraordinary expertise that birds display whilst creating these architectural and engineering marvels … with their beaks!

Materials

Take your time to collect materials and think about the things a bird might use to make a nest … twigs, leaves, moss, feathers, mud, grasses, cobwebs, animal fur and even man-made materials like string and cloth.

You may spot a real bird's nest as you are exploring. Have a look from a distance and take notes from a master builder!

Get building

I'm not going to give prescriptive instructions for this one; it's time to experiment, get your hands dirty, weave and knit that structure together. Watch it fall apart and then find a way to keep it together. Relax and enjoy!

BIG birds

Could you build a human-sized nest? It makes a great snug with a tent, blanket and some books.

26

Stick art

Making land art using sticks and natural materials is one of my favourite ways to spend time. It is creative, relaxing, meditative, stimulating and hugely satisfying. There is a beauty and a truth to its ephemeral nature; here for a time, then dispersed by weather and animals.

I created this piece with the brilliant artist James Brunt. There are many ways to approach land art; this is just one of them. So, rather than a strict set of instructions to follow, think of these pages as an invitation to venture out and have a go. Enjoy!

1. Walk until you find the right place and materials. Don't rush this bit or despair if you don't find somewhere instantly – the right place will make itself known to you. You might wish to choose a spot next to a natural feature such as a tree, roots or a riverbank. Magical things happen when land art interacts with the landscape.

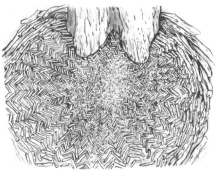

2. It all starts with one stick! Start a pattern and continue outwards. Carry on and lose yourself in the design. Try not to worry about small imperfections – the viewer's eye will correct them as they gaze at it.

3. Don't be afraid to change the pattern as your stick art grows. Stand back from time to time to get a view of the whole piece. At some point, your piece will let you know that it's time to stop tinkering and it's finished.

Again, this is just one way to approach making land art – try making paths, literal or abstract designs, goddesses, a Green Man, or play with working vertically and up into the trees.

Stick play

Take some time from your busy life to play. That's right – play! It's not just for children, although these activities work really well with little people. A stick offers an infinite number of possibilities – here are some of my favourites.

27

Skipping rope

Beloved by snotty schoolchildren and burly boxers alike, the humble skipping rope is always a winner. Make your own in the woods using this simple guide.

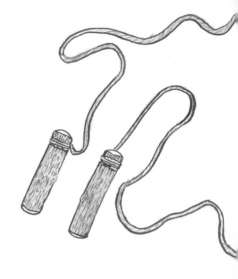

1. Find (or cut) two sticks for the handles that are the desired weight and size. A good rule of thumb is around 10cm in length for a child and 15cm for an adult. The diameter should be about 3cm.

2. Use the stop cut and thumb push stroke techniques (page 27) to create a lovely little groove in which you can tie off the rope. Use your knife or sandpaper to smooth the ends and edges of the handles. You could also use your knife to make decorative patterns.

3. Cut your rope or cordage to size. You could use sisal, paracord or even natural cordage. For a child, use a rope around 1.5–2m long, moving up to around 3m for a taller adult. Fasten each end to the handles using a clove hitch followed by a half hitch (page 30) and skip to your heart's content.

28

Catapult

Is there a greater joy than closing one eye to take aim, stretching back that arm and watching as your catapult sends its missile hurtling towards the target?

You can experiment with different projectiles, but be careful where you fire that thing. Never aim the catapult at people or animals.

1. Find a Y-shaped, hardwood branch no thinner than 2cm in diameter and cut it to size. The greener (fresher) the better, so keep your eye out when a mature tree drops a big branch – the perfect catapult stick might have fallen at your feet!

2. Use your knife to cut a notch around 1–2cm from the top of each arm. Smooth the edges of both arms and the handle with sandpaper. You could even strip the bark or carve designs into your catapult.

3. Get your sling ready. For an adult-sized catapult, the sling should be around 45cm long. You could use a ready-made rubber sling with a leather pouch in the middle. Alternatively, you could use two 25cm lengths of surgical tubing (or anything springy) and create a pouch from an old leather belt. Cut a belt section that includes two holes and tie it to the tubing using the technique described in step 4.

4. Ask a friend to help you with this bit. One of you will hold the rubber around the notch (keep the leather pouch on the outside if you're using a ready-made sling). The other will tie the rubber in place using dental floss. (Yes, really!) You could also use the fine inner threads from paracord (page 29) for this task. If you're making your own sling, tie the pouch to each end of the tubing. Your catapult is finished.

29

Rope swing

Ah, the simple attraction of a rope swing. They bring so much joy and are incredibly easy to set up when you know how.

A few important safety considerations: choose a space free of dangerous objects within the swinging zone, both on the ground and in the air. Make sure all trees and branches that you use are living and can support the weight of your rope swingers. Your rope should be 12–16mm thick, in good condition and graded as 'weight bearing'.

1. Choose your tree and swing branch. The branch could be just 2m high for a swing for young children or higher for older children and adults.

2. Throw a rope over the swing branch and tie an alpine butterfly knot (page 33) in the middle, leaving at least enough rope on one side to go from your chosen branch to the ground. Make the loop roughly as big as your hand.

3. Pull the end of the rope through the loop and keep pulling until the loop has risen to the branch; this will be the end to which you will attach the swing. Tie the other end of the rope to the trunk or a nearby living tree using a timber hitch (page 33).

4. Find (or cut) a 40cm length of wood that can hold your weight, then use a clove hitch (page 30) finished with a half hitch (page 30) to attach it to the rope. Make sure the height of the seat allows people using the swing to get on and off unaided. Now get swinging!

To take the rope down, simply untie all knots at ground level and pull down from the end that was attached to the tree trunk.

30

Zip line

I've loved this zip line set-up ever since its creator, outdoor educator Baba Lafene, introduced me to it. You're going to love it too.

As with the rope swing on the previous pages, choose a space free of dangerous objects, both on the ground and in the air. Make sure all trees and branches that you use are living and can support the weight of your zip-liners.

Equipment needed

NOTE: All items should be rated for climbing use to ensure strength and safety.

2 × 22-mm tape sling (1 × 1.2m, 1 × 1.5m)
3 × swing cheek pulley for 12-mm or 13-mm rope
(I like the pulley to be a little big for the rope)
3 × steel carabiner (screw gate or auto lock)
1 × static 11-mm or 12-mm rope, 30m in length

TARGET
TREE

STARTING
TREE

1. Choose your two trees: the starting tree and the target tree (page 97). There should be 7–15m of clear space between your starting and target tree. In the starting tree, use square lashing (page 32) and a sturdy branch to build a stable platform around 2–3m off the ground. You will need to be able to climb up to the platform safely using branches or a ladder (page 128).

Stand on the platform and use a running bowline (page 31) to attach the rope as high as you can reach on your starting tree. Tie the other end of the rope off temporarily on the target tree while you work on step 2.

2. Use a lark's foot (page 31) to attach the 1.5-m sling around the target tree, 20cm–1.5m from the base depending on the angle you want for your zip line. Take the rope, attach a pulley and connect to the sling using a carabiner.

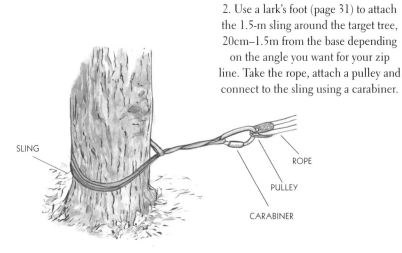

SLING

ROPE

PULLEY

CARABINER

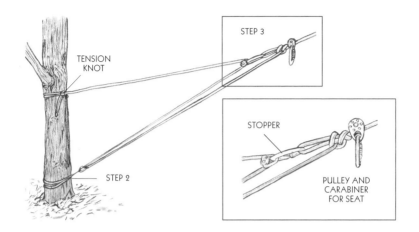

TENSION KNOT

STEP 3

STOPPER

STEP 2

PULLEY AND CARABINER FOR SEAT

3. Now we will create our stopper –
the point at which the zip line will
halt before the rider hits the ground –
normally between 1.5m and 3m from
the target tree.

Tie an alpine butterfly knot (page
33) to create a loop and then attach a
pulley and carabiner to the rope above
the knot. This pulley will hold the seat
we build in step 4.

Attach a carabiner and pulley to the
alpine butterfly loop, then pull the end
of the rope through the pulley and tie
it off as tightly as you can on the target
tree, at around chest height, using a
tension knot (page 30).

4. Find (or cut) a strong length of
wood around 40cm long. Fasten the
1.2cm sling to the carabiner and seat
with two lark's foot knots on the bight
(page 31). Check you are happy with
the seat height and get going!

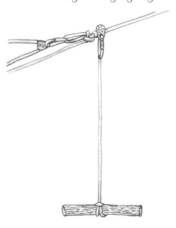

31

Drum stalks

A simple and repetitive drum rhythm has the potential to evoke an ancient feeling within us. These pages invite you to use these rhythms to connect with the natural world and give space to your playful side.

In each of these games, players must make their way towards the drummer by following their rhythm. Use two sticks against a bigger log to make your drumbeats.

Experiment with different sticks until you are happy with the timbre (the quality or tone of the sound). You could also beat your sticks against a bucket, barrel or drum. Try using your hands to create different rhythms too.

Drum stalk

The drummer sits at one end of the playing area while the group
begin at the agreed start tree, 20–40m behind the drummer in a
wooded area. When the drummer makes the rhythm, which is
around 5 seconds long and the same every time, it is time for the
group to sneak towards the drummer.

When the drummer is not drumming, they turn around and call
out the names of the people they can see. If your name is called,
you go back to the start tree and go again on the next rhythm. The
aim of the game is to reach the drummer without being sent back.

Boomshakalaka

I love this game! It is a cross between the drum stalk and the
classic Capture the Flag. Players split into two teams and a flag is
placed behind the drummer. The rules are the same as the drum
stalk, but this time each team must try to retrieve the flag from
behind the drummer and make it back to the start tree without
being seen. If a player is spotted with the flag, they must put it
back behind the drummer and return to the start tree. You can
keep score and the team with the most points wins!

Blindfolded drum stalk

Participants spread out across the area and are blindfolded. (It's good to start this game in a field or open space and progress to more challenging terrain.)

The drummer beats the rhythm with regular gaps of silence and participants make their way towards the sound at their own pace. Helpers support the blindfolded participants when they might bump into a tree or object. The aim is to follow the rhythms and find the drummer – participants learn to trust themselves and their senses along the way.

Go barefoot

When it is safe to do so, participants are encouraged to play barefoot to help them feel grounded – and for sensory loveliness!

32

Stick games

There are so many games that you can play with sticks, here are just a few! Try inventing your own too.

That's not a stick!

A game of mime similar to charades, this one is great for getting the mind whirring about the many possibilities for imaginative play with a single stick.

Each person goes away and finds a stick that reminds them of another object (e.g. toothbrush, saxophone, moustache etc). They then come back to the group and mime an action associated with their chosen object (e.g. brushing teeth, playing a song etc). To take a guess, the group shout: 'That's not a stick! It's a …'

Noughts and crosses

It's a classic! Create a three-by-three grid. Two players take turns marking the spaces with an 'X' or 'O'. The aim of the game is to get three of your symbols in a row.

Pick-up sticks

Make a jumbled pile of sticks of similar length. Players take turns carefully pulling sticks out without making any others move. Each player picks out as many sticks as they can until the pile moves, then it's the next player's turn. At the end, the winner is the person who has collected the most sticks.

Blowpipe

The blowpipe is another great use for the magical elder tree (page 12) and its soft, pithy centre that is so easily hollowed out.

Make your pipe

Find a length of elder and use a tent peg or stick to hollow out the centre.

Now let's think about what to use your blowpipe for …

Shooting

Use your pipe to shoot little projectiles like seeds or berries; take care to avoid anything toxic and agree with the group where you will fire them.

Leaf race

Pick up objects by sucking rather than blowing. Get two lines of people and race to see who can pass the leaf along the entire row first.

Make a maze

Make a maze with sticks and blow an object around it – maybe an empty snail shell or berry. Or make a mini football field and blow the 'ball' to score a goal.

Fire bellows

Choose a longer length of elder, and push the pith out with wire to create a pipe to breathe life into your fire!

34

Magic wand

Every wizard needs a wand. It's
time to go and find yours.

Please use your wand (and the
magic it holds) responsibly!

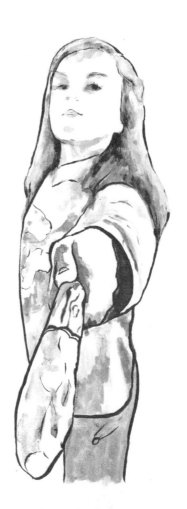

Let your wand find you

Take a walk and keep your eyes open for that special stick that
has been waiting just for you. Indeed, as they say, 'the wand
chooses the wizard.'

Your wand might be a delightfully wonky, knobbly bit of wood,
or it could be straight as an arrow. You'll know when you meet it.

Which wood?

It is said that Merlin, the great wizard from the Arthurian tales, used
a wand of English oak. Harry Potter famously used a holly wand.
You may choose to read up on the lore surrounding wand woods …
or simply let the wand find you. What wood will yours be?

Personalizing

Will you choose to carve designs into the handle and shaft
(children, please do so with the support of an adult), or will
you strip the bark completely?

Will you attach any other items to your wand? If you can find a
dragon's tooth, phoenix feather or piece of unicorn horn, all the
better, but don't worry too much if these are not available
in your local woodland.

Obstacle course

Obstacle courses are not just for kids! Monkeying around on rope bridges, beams, ladders and the like is good for the development of balance, strength, agility and risk judgement – as well as a lot of fun.

Whether you are a parkour master perfecting your 'double corkscrew' or a toddler tumbling around, a few of these ideas can help you turn the woods into your very own adventure playground.

Make sure all trees you build on are living and can support the weight of your constructions. Always supervise children and young people when building and enjoying the obstacle course.

Let's get building!

Beams and ladders

Use square lashing (page 32) and lengths of green (fresh) wood to create ladders. (See page 128 for more details.) Use the same lashing skills to add high bars to swing on and beams to vault. Balance on and walk along your beams and bars too!

TIMBER HITCH
(TIE FIRST)

TENSION
KNOT

Ropes

Use a timber hitch and tension knot (pages 33 and 30) to create a single line to climb up or down, or put up two parallel ropes together to create a bridge, as pictured.

You could also add a rope swing (page 94) or zip line (page 96). You are the architect of this woodland playground; and it can look just as you want!

36

Frog stick

This is a forest version of the Puerto Rican instrument, the güiro. Rub your beater along the frog stick to get that authentic 'ribbit' sound and add some froggy vibes to your woodland percussion crew!

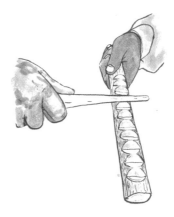

1. Find a straight branch of hardwood around 30cm long. Using a knife or saw, make a series of stop cuts on one side of the stick, working at regular intervals and cutting away from you. Each cut should be around 1cm deep. Then use a thumb push stroke to make diagonal cuts all the way along your frog stick. (See page 27 for techniques.)

2. Turn the stick around and repeat in the other direction to create a series of V-shaped ridges along the top of your frog stick.

3. Create a beater with another stick by whittling away to create a sharp edge on one side. Now get playing … it's time to dance!

37

Story stick

This is a lovely activity that invites us to move more mindfully through the landscape, collecting items along the way to create our own personal and unique record of the journey. The story stick then becomes an opportunity to recount the experience or encourage more imaginative storytelling if that feels right for the group.

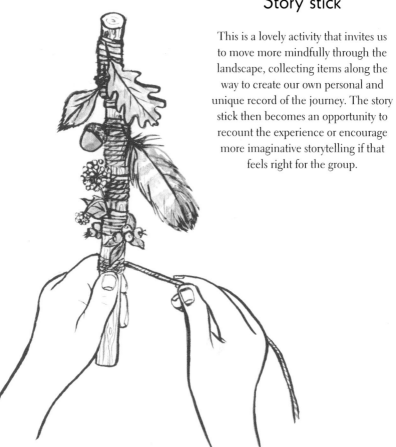

1. Choose a stick that you can comfortably carry. Next grab
some bits of string, coloured yarn or natural cordage and head
out on your journey. Smaller children could use rubber bands
or sticky tape, but please don't leave any litter behind.

2. As you walk, really try to notice what is around you. Use all
of your senses. Feel free to slow down and stop whenever you
are drawn to do so.

3. Select natural items to reflect the different stages of your
journey and tie these onto your stick. You might choose leaves,
feathers, seeds, flowers or anything else you might find – there is
no right or wrong.

Remember: only take one of each and only choose things that
are in abundance. Consider giving gratitude to the plant or place
that gifts you each item.

Once your group is back together, you may choose to share
your story sticks and use them to tell the tale of your
journey, the places you've been and how you felt
along the way.

Camp sticks

Whether camping out or looking for a cool project to try in the woods, this section will help you improve your camp craft and your woodland set-up!

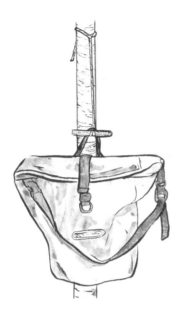

38

Woodland coat hanger

This easy project is a great way to hang bags, coats and hats in the woods. It will keep them off the ground in a naturally sheltered spot under the tree's canopy, and your camp will be nice and tidy.

1. Use a timber hitch (page 33) to attach a length of string to your tree, leaving at least 20cm of string hanging in front of you.

2. Use a lark's foot knot (page 31) to tie a small stick – about 8–15cm in length – to the hanging end of your string.

And that's it! It really is that simple. You're ready to hang whatever you like on there.

39

Measure a tree

This is such a neat little technique to estimate the height of a tree. All you need is a stick!

1. Find a stick that is the same length as the distance between your hand and your eye when your arm is outstretched in front of you.

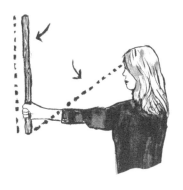

2. Stand in line with the tree. Hold the stick vertically and stretch out your arm in front of you. Walk backwards away from the tree, taking care as you do so. Stop when the top of the stick in your outstretched arm lines up with the top of the tree; this is the point where the top of the tree would land if it had been felled and fell in front of you.

3. Measure the distance back to the tree by counting your steps as you walk in a straight line back to its base.

Most people's stride length (the distance travelled in each step) is 0.4 × their height. So, if you are 1.5m tall, your stride will be 60cm.

If you multiply the number of steps by the length of your stride, you can estimate the height of the tree!

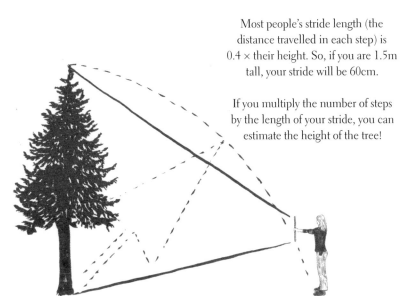

40

Tracking stick

A tracking stick is a simple tool to help you follow the tracks of an animal. The thing I like most about this skill is that it slows us down and makes us pay attention to the ground and what's down there. I may never make the best tracker as I am forever distracted by the magical world of minibeasts, moss and mushrooms.

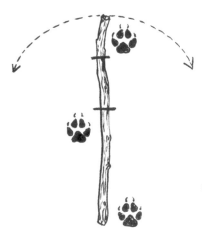

1. Find a straight stick and locate the footprint of the animal you are tracking. Put the top end of your stick in line with the top of a print. Using a knife, some mud or charcoal, mark the back of that print and the top of the print behind it. Your stick now shows the stride of the animal and the length of its footprint.

2. Most animals' stride lengths are similar on different terrains and when walking or running. So even when it seems the trail has 'disappeared', you can use the stick to make a sweeping motion (above ground to avoid disturbing signs on the floor) to find subsequent prints and continue to track the animal.

A note on tracking humans

We track humans heel-to-heel rather than toe-to-toe; this is because we tend to strike the ground with our heels rather than the balls of our feet (as animals do). This means that the heel print is often the easiest to spot when trailing a human.

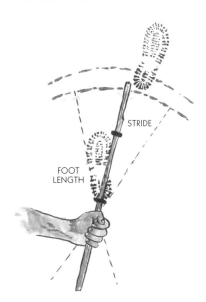

STRIDE

FOOT
LENGTH

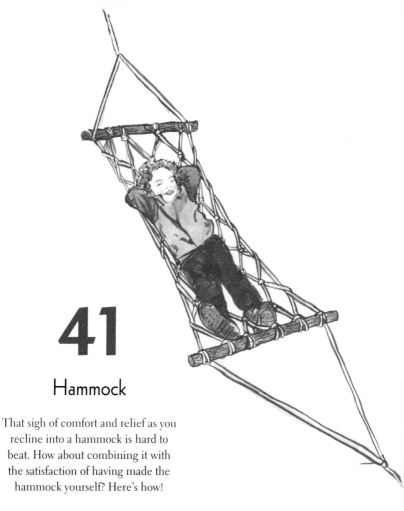

41

Hammock

That sigh of comfort and relief as you recline into a hammock is hard to beat. How about combining it with the satisfaction of having made the hammock yourself? Here's how!

A note on which rope to use: for hammocks, I like a 6–8mm soft cotton braided rope, as it is easy to work with and tie (particularly whilst making the netting) and feels lovely to lie on.

1. Start with one length of rope and two sturdy sticks of green (fresh) wood, at least 3cm in diameter. For an adult hammock, use 9m of rope and sticks 0.8–1m in length. For a child's hammock, go for 5m of rope and sticks that are 60–80cm long.

2. Use a clove hitch (page 30) to attach the rope to each end of the sticks, leaving at least 1m of rope as loops on either side.

3. Use the netting technique shown on page 33 to create your comfy hammock bed. For this, cut at least four lengths of rope – each one should be six times as long as the distance between the sticks.

Making the netting will be easiest if you suspend the hammock structure between two trees at a comfortable working height. You could hang it up directly using the loops at each end or add additional lengths of rope to reach your hanging points using a tension knot (page 30). Make sure the trees to which you attach the hammock are strong enough to hold a person's weight.

4. Turn your phone off and grab a drink and some snacks. See you in a couple of hours …

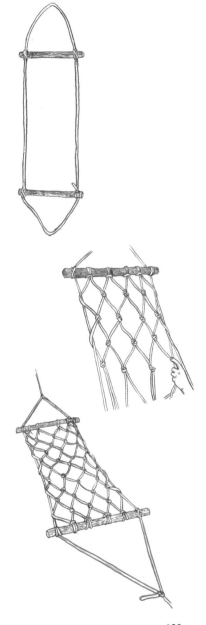

42

Three-legged stool

This little tripod or milking stool is quick and easy. You can also make one with four legs, although the beauty of a tripod is that the three legs will always settle into a free-standing position.

1. Find a length of hardwood around 40cm long and 20cm in diameter. Use an axe or froe to split it just off-centre to create a flat edge on one side – this will be the seat of your stool. You could smooth the top and edges with a knife, drawknife or sandpaper at this point.

2. Take a 2.5-cm Scotch-eyed auger (page 25) or other drilling tool and brace. Then drill three 7-cm deep holes, each at a slight angle away from the others, in a triangle formation on the rounded side of the wood.

3. Cut three straight rods of hardwood with a diameter of around 3.5cm – the ends should be just too wide to fit in the holes. The length of the legs will set the height of your stool, so consider if your stool is for someone tall or short.

Whittle down the ends, a little bit at a time, until they are still just a millimetre or two too wide for the holes. If the legs slide in easily the stool will not stay together.

4. Use a mallet to drive the three legs into the sockets. You may need to stop to shave just a little more off the legs between strikes. Flip it to stand on its legs and you are done!

43

Stake bench

Make a bench in the woods with this simple guide.

1. Cut four stakes – these will be the vertical poles at each corner of your bench. They should be made of straight, green (fresh) wood at least 1m long and 4–6cm in diameter for an adult-sized bench. Whittle each stake to a point at one end.

Alternatively, you could use a standing tree for your uprights, as I have done in the example on page 127.

If your bench is longer than 1.2m, you may wish to add two central stakes for additional support.

2. Cut two lengths of green (fresh) wood 20cm longer than the length you would like your bench to be. Drive your stakes into the ground using a large mallet or log. Use square lashing (page 32) to attach the lengths to the stakes (or standing tree/s) at a right angle.

3. Now it's time to saw and lay out poles on top of the bench for the seat. Each should be at least 15cm longer than the width of your bench and at least 2cm in diameter. You will need a lot of them so allow time for this bit!

4. Fasten them to the bench frame starting with a clove hitch (page 30), tightly threading your cordage diagonally around each stick as shown in figure 1 before finishing with another clove hitch.

5. Trim and straighten the edges with a saw and you are finished.

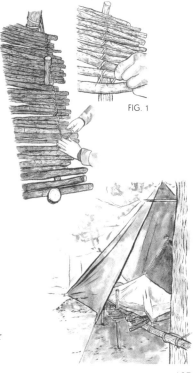

FIG. 1

You may also choose to put a tarpaulin up and use your stake bench as a bed for the night!

44

Stick ladders

Making ladders in the woods is a lot of fun and a useful skill too. You can build them for play structures (page 110) or practical purposes such as construction or harvesting fruit.

Lashed ladder

1. Cut two long rails and as many steps as you need from green (fresh) wood. Lay them on the ground and check your ladder is the desired length and width.

2. Use square lashing (page 32) to fasten the steps to the side rails with cordage at least 3mm thick.

Hanging rope ladder

1. Cut one length of weight-bearing rope to at least six times the length that you would like your ladder to be.

2. Saw (or find) strong, straight sticks around 40–50cm in length for the steps.

3. Fold the rope in half and hang it over a branch.

4. Use a clove hitch on a bight (page 30) to attach the steps to the rope at regular intervals. You can lift your ladder and move it around as you wish.

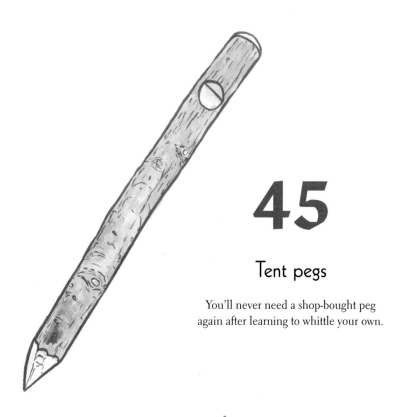

45

Tent pegs

You'll never need a shop-bought peg again after learning to whittle your own.

1. Find (or saw) a length of green (fresh) wood that is between 20cm and 40cm long. Use a knife to whittle one end to a point.

FIG. 1

FIG. 2

2. Create a neat groove for the guy lines with a stop cut (figure 1) and a thumb push stroke (figure 2). See page 27 for more details on these techniques.

3. Now use your knife to bevel the sharp edges at the thicker end of the peg. This will create a rounded top and stop the peg from splitting when it is driven into the ground with a mallet.

Tips

- Make longer pegs and drive them deeper into the ground on windier days. Use more pegs and guy lines too!

- Angle your peg away from the tent or tarpaulin structure when beating it into the ground.

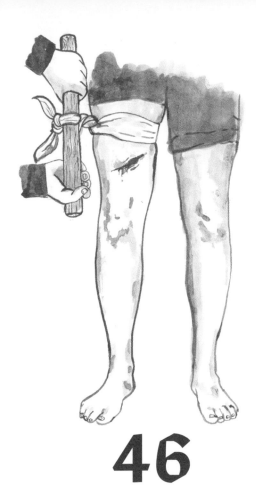

46

Emergency sticks

As well as the playful, creative and practical applications of sticks elsewhere in this book, the humble branch can also play a vital role in an emergency, allowing us to preserve life and prevent deterioration in the condition of a casualty while they await expert treatment.

Tourniquet

Where there is bleeding on a limb, wrap a length of non-stretchy fabric (a torn shirt or long sock could work) 5–10cm above the wound and twist a stick into the excess fabric as tightly as you can to restrict blood flow from the heart to the wound. Secure your tourniquet with a second strip of fabric, or by tucking it into the existing wrap.

Splint

Make a splint to restrict the movement of an injured area with a stick or two, fastened in place with tape, string or fabric.

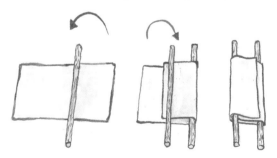

Stretcher

This is an ingenious method for creating a stretcher using two sticks and a tarpaulin or blanket. It can also be useful for transporting things around a camp or woodland site. Fold as shown on the diagram. No bindings are needed – the weight of the casualty or cargo will hold it in place.

47

Tripod shelter

This is a really cool design for a day shelter (rather than a
survival structure) and it comes complete with a hanger so your
kettle or pot can sit above the fire. Build one and spend some
good time out in the wild, listening to your thoughts and the
sounds of the natural world.

1. Let's make the tripod structure. Find two lengths of wood 2–3m long and another that's roughly double that length. Lay the poles on the ground and use the tripod lashing technique (page 32) to bind them together at least 20cm from the ends.

2. Lift and stand your tripod as shown here.

3. Attach your tarpaulin to the apex of the tripod, either side of the entrance, and at a spot around 2–3m behind it with string and pegs (page 130). You may also wish to use your tarpaulin to create a groundsheet below you.

4. Use square lashing (page 32) to attach a hooked branch to the structure, 1–2m in front of your shelter. Light your fire and hang a pot on there. While it bubbles away, maybe it's time to make the stick bread on the following pages …

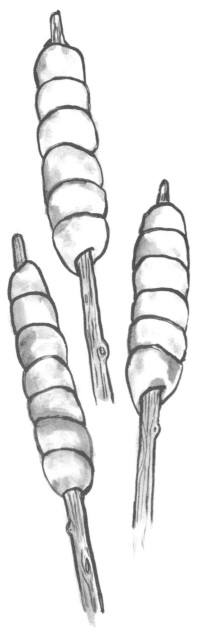

48

Stick bread

This is my recipe for a delicious bready treat on the campfire, with no measurements and no nonsense! It's fun to experiment with adding ingredients into your dough too – how about foraged herbs or cheese for a savoury stick bread? Or sugar and cinnamon for the sweet-toothed? You're going to love it.

1. Find long, straight sticks – any non-toxic wood will do. Hazel works well as it grows naturally in long, straight lengths. Strip the bark off the end of the stick. Oh, and get the fire lit too – you'll be cooking over the embers, not leaping flames.

2. It's time to make the dough. Wash your hands. Then mix two mugs of flour and a big pinch of salt in a big bowl. Pour in a tablespoon of olive oil and a splash of cold water and mix with your hands. Knead, adding a little more water if necessary, until you have a smooth, firm dough. A teaspoon of sugar, a tablespoon of baking powder and/or an egg can also be nice additions to this, as can other non-wheat flours, so get experimenting.

3. Dust your hands in flour and roll the dough into little balls. Stretch one into a long, thin sausage shape and twist it around the bark-free end of your stick, leaving small gaps and pinching the dough together at the bottom. Hold it over the glowing embers and rotate your stick to get a nice and even brown crust on the outside.

4. Tear your bread off in strips and dip it in yoghurt, jam or chocolate spread. Or you could slide the bread off whole and put a sausage in the middle!

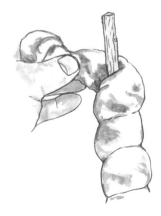

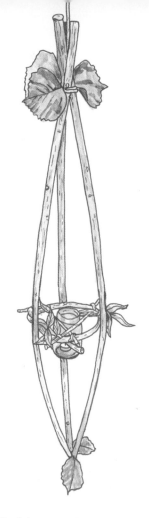

49

Stretch lantern

These lanterns are beautiful and surprisingly simple to create. Whether a single lantern in the garden or a whole line guiding you deeper into the woods at dusk, they never fail to impress.

1. Find three straight rods of green (fresh) wood around 2–3cm in diameter and 1–1.5m in length. Hazel works well. Use a clove hitch and a half hitch (page 30) to tie them together tightly about 15–20cm from each end.

2. Cut a 1m length of bendy willow branch and shape it into a ring. Slide the ring into the centre of the three branches from step 1 (see left). Make sure the ring is wedged nice and securely in there.

This is good time to hang the lantern from a tree.

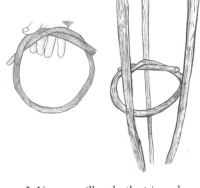

3. Now we will make the triangular structure that will sit in the ring and hold a jam jar for our candle.

Find another three sticks of green (fresh) willow around 25cm long and thin one end of each stick with a knife.

4. Push the tip of your knife into the branch around 5cm from the opposite end and twist the knife. This will create an opening into which you can slide the shaved end of the other sticks, creating a triangle structure.

5. Sit your triangle on top of the ring and place your jam jar inside, adjusting it so the jar is nice and snug. Then you can decorate your lantern using natural materials.

As the light fades, light the candle and admire your work ...

50

Bark knife sheath

This knife sheath uses the same sweet chestnut bark as the pot (page 56). You could also use cedar, birch, elm or willow bark. You can read more about harvesting, preparing and soaking bark on page 16.

For this design, we'll need four 1.2 × 60cm strips of bark. This will give us a sheath about 3cm wide and 15cm long. You can make a larger sheath or even a wall basket using the same method; simply increase the width or number of strips.

1. Take four strips of soaked bark and fold them in half precisely. Mark the midpoint on each and weave them together as shown here.

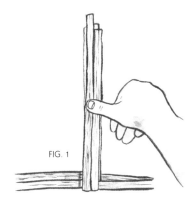

FIG. 1

2. Fold over two of the strips that are next to each other to form a T-shape (figure 1). Now fold in the other strips, alternating under and over as shown in figure 2. This will form the pointed section at the bottom of the sheath.

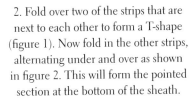

FIG. 2

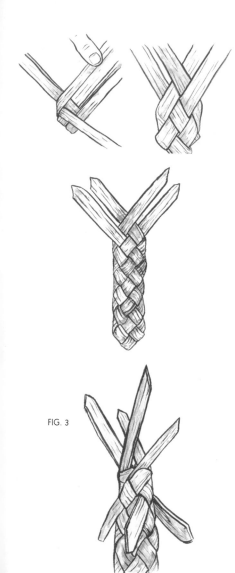

FIG. 3

3. Turn the weave so the point of the sheath is facing you. Then take the left strip and fold it over. Next, fold the exposed strip diagonally upwards at a 45-degree angle and weave it in and out of each strip it meets. Turn the weave over and do the same to the strip that was folded back that is now on the right.

Begin this process again from what is now the left side and repeat until you have reached your desired length, or there is only 5cm of strip left at the top.

4. Cut the ends to a point and fold down at a 45-degree angle. This should give you a flat 'top' to the folded strips and they will align with the weave of the sheath. Tuck them into the weave below, as in figure 3. You might need to open the sheath with your finger when bending the strips round the flat corners.

Carefully snip the ends above and below the rim and place your knife into the sheath (it should be a tight fit) while it dries overnight.

Sources

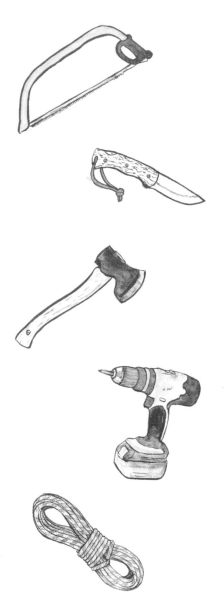

Gear

Rope and cordage: rope-source.co.uk,
ropesandtwines.com

Climbing equipment including static
ropes: honeybros.com

550 paracord: paracord.eu

Tarpaulins and hammocks:
ddhammocks.com

Tools

Knives, including spoon/hook knives:
morakniv.se, benandloisorford.com

Axes: gransforsbruk.com

Folding/pruning saw: silkysaws.com

Bow saw and loppers: bahco.com

Secateurs: niwaki.com

Froe, drawknife: oldtoolstore.co.uk,
gransforsbruk.com

Scotch-eyed auger and bit and brace
set: look for these on second-hand sites
online and old tool stores.

Multitool: leatherman.co.uk,
victorinox.com

Electric drill: makitauk.com

Tool sharpening:
woodsmithexperience.co.uk

Acknowledgements

The deepest gratitude and acknowledgement to the people who contributed directly and indirectly to this book: Patrick Harrison, Maria Sprostranova, Marnie Rose and The Garden Classroom, Mollie and Nick McMillen, James Brunt, George Mayfield, Millie Darling, Adam Njenga, Ruth Ferguson, Viv and Mia Rowdon, Ria Knowles, Amy Haworth, Holly Jacks, Jon Cree, Lily Horseman, Tim Rowe-Horseman, Baba Lafene, Rebecca Card, Marley, Sonny, Hazel, Ted, Greta, Lyra, Ed, Big Mike, Magz, October '21 TGC L3 cohort, Duncan and Alice, Jonny, Chris, Nigelito, TB, Woody, Pez, my BCN and Vinaixa family, Rhiannon and Kinship in Nature, Jo and London Green Wood, Lizzy and Forest Grove, and Ellen Vellacot and the Super Roots crew.

Huge appreciation and respect for Maria for her wonderful illustrations, and Clare Double, Krissy Mallett and the team at Pavilion for steering the project from inception to publication.

Finally, my eternal thanks and love to Roxanne, Santi and Zia – my favourite adventurers.

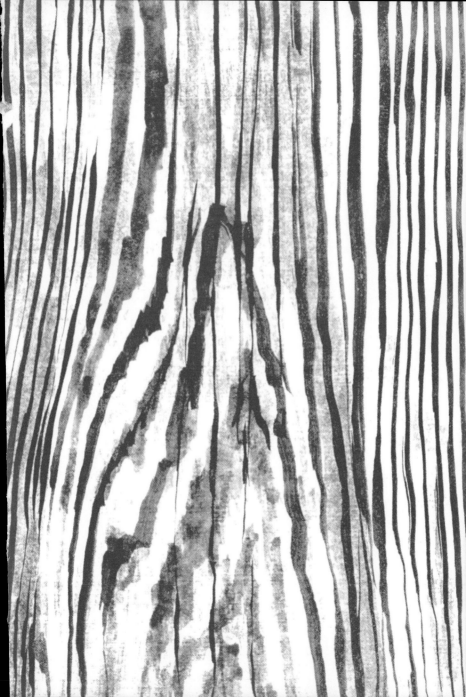

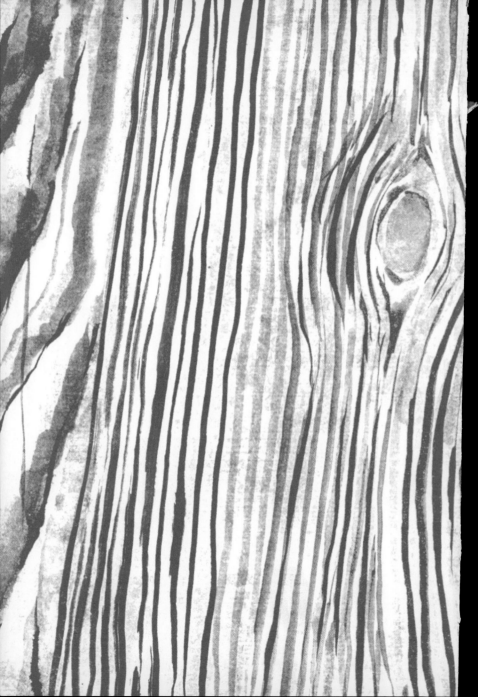